The Art of Youth Work
Kerry Young

Russell House Publishing

First published in 1999 by:
Russell House Publishing Ltd.
4 St. George's House
Uplyme Road
Lyme Regis
Dorset DT7 3LS

Tel. 01297-443948
Fax. 01297 442722
e-mail help@russellhouse.co.uk

© Kerry Young

British Library Cataloguing-in-publication Data:
A catalogue record for this book is available from the British Library.

ISBN: 1-898924-49-X

Typeset by The Hallamshire Press Limited, Sheffield.

Printed by Cromwell Press, Trowbridge.

Russell House Publishing
Is a group of social work, probation, education and community work practitioners
working in collaboration with a professional publishing team. Our aim is to work
closely with the field to produce innovative and valuable materials to help managers,
trainers, practitioners and students. We are keen to receive feedback on publications
and new ideas for future projects.

About the author

Kerry Young has been involved in youth work since 1977 as a detached youth worker and, later, national officer at the National Youth Bureau, National Association of Youth Clubs (now Youth Clubs UK) and the National Youth Agency. She is now an independent consultant and associate of the Youth Affairs Unit at De Montfort University, Leicester.

If you would like to discuss the perspectives offered in this book or share your thinking about the future directions for youth work and the youth service, you can contact Kerry via her e-mail: kerryyoung@compuserve.com

Acknowledgements

This book would never have been produced without the time, commitment and support of a huge number of people.

Firstly, the 32 youth workers and young people who allowed themselves to be interviewed and who shared their thinking and experiences with warmth, openness, honesty and integrity.

Secondly, Dr. Neil Kendra, Yvonne Field and Amanda Harrington whose time, patience and invaluable comments helped to create the text you are about to read.

Finally, the National Youth Agency for allowing me to use interview material I originally produced for the report on the 1996–99 Youth Work Development Grants Programme.

Thank you.

Contents

A brief note about methodology

This book is based on a collection of interviews with youth workers and young people across England, Wales and Northern Ireland. This includes 32 individuals, 16 of whom are main contributors insofar as I specifically arranged to interview them, and their interviews represent a substantial part of the text. The other 16 are workers and young people whom I met, more briefly, as a result of my visits to different centres and projects.

The 16 main contributors were either previously known to me or contacted via:

● The Youth and Policy History Conference (November 1998)

● a letter in *Young People Now* magazine (December 1998)

● other workers involved in the book

Individual interviews were taped and the transcripts edited, by me, to create thematic quotations which were then amended and approved by each interviewee. Interviewees were also given the opportunity to comment on the first draft of the book if they so wished.

Quotations are not generally attributed to specific individuals although some connections may be obvious by virtue of their content. However, the contributors to this book should not remain entirely anonymous. Each has made his or her distinctive contribution arising from her or his own experience, identity and concerns about youth work. Therefore, in order to illuminate where each person is 'coming from', the book contains one extended quotation ascribed to each of the main contributors.

It is also important to note that the perspectives offered and observations made are strictly the personal opinion of the individuals involved. As such, they do not necessarily represent the policy or position of any youth and community service or voluntary organisation by whom the individual may be employed.

This book was created in this way for three main reasons:

● Firstly, discussions about youth work purpose and practice are not easy. In the end one is inevitably faced with the question 'what do youth workers do?' Therefore, the only way to make the discussion 'real' is to provide actual descriptions of practice - real people talking about what they actually do.

● Secondly, the quotations from youth workers and young people provide vivid demonstrations of the fact that the kind of youth work being envisioned in this book is already taking place. Not in a narrow or restricted way but in a wide variety of familiar settings and contexts; with many different kinds of young people. Indeed, the breadth of practice reflected here is only eclipsed by the amazing consistency of workers' sense of purpose and underpinning values.

- Thirdly, the large collection of direct quotations from workers and young people reflects a commitment to preserving their authentic 'voice' and, importantly, reflecting their essential meanings since it is through narratives that human existence is rendered meaningful. (Cortazzi 1993). Therefore, contributors' own words provide a means for understanding the meaning they have given to their own experiences and reflections.

Contributors

Michael Clarke is a youth worker of long standing with a range of experiences in different youth work settings. He is currently involved with a detached project in an inner city area of Manchester, where some of the most challenging aspects of work with young people are currently taking place.

Kevin Crawford has experienced the youth and community service as a young person, volunteer, worker and manager since the sixties. In his view, the service has provided him with a wide range of opportunities which have significantly affected his personal development and the values that he holds today.

Teresa Geraghty is a professionally qualified youth worker, originally from the Republic of Ireland, now living in Belfast, where she works with the Children's Law Centre as a researcher. Research and professional interests include young people's rights, community development and work with young people in rural areas. She is co-author of 'A Sense of Belonging' – a research report on the needs and aspirations of young people in rural areas of Northern Ireland.

Abdul Ghaffar was born in Pakistan, came to Britain in 1967 and grew up in Saltley, an inner city area of Birmingham. He qualified as a youth and community worker in 1987, and has worked in both local authority youth and community services and voluntary organisations. He currently works with Sparkhill Youth Project, a detached youth work project in Birmingham. He has been instrumental in carrying out innovative and pioneering sustainable developmental youth work.

Mo Hand has been a youth worker and project manager in London and Bristol for the past 19 years. The majority of her work has been in developing and supporting lesbian and gay youth provision around the country. She is also a freelance trainer and consultant on equal opportunities issues.

Ella Jess has been working with young African people for over 21 years. She currently works for Lambeth Youth Service where, with colleague Paul Reid, she has pioneered an Africentric approach to work with young Black people. She is an associate trainer of Khepera Management and Training (KMT), a training agency specialising in Africentric solutions to Eurocentric problems. Ella is a proud mother of two and mentor to many.

Jennie Lamb is a Development Manager at the Guide Association, the largest youth organisation in the UK. She is responsible for adult support and, as such, her role includes the review and development of a range of training strategies, from basic leadership to training and development NVQs. Jenny is also a member of the NCVYS training strategies group and the National Youth Agency Education and Training Standards (ETS) sub-committee.

Paul Mattis is a member of a detached project team in an inner city area of Manchester, where his main emphasis is the development of strategies and approaches to assist young people to address their negative attitudes and activities. He is also currently undertaking professional qualifying training at Manchester Metropolitan University.

Kevin Murphy has been a teacher and youth worker for 25 years in Oxford, Liverpool, Potters Bar and Humberside. In Nottinghamshire he developed a mobile rural youth work scheme which achieved national recognition. He is committed to generic social education for all young people. Circus skills are his favourite 'tool'.

Ann Robinson has been a part-time youth worker for 17 years. During this time she has worked with young people around a range of issues, including homelessness and sexuality. For a number of years, the majority of her work has been with young people with disabilities, and particularly with young people experiencing a learning disability.

John Rose is the Assistant Director of the Wales Youth Agency. In the last three years he has been actively involved in developing and promoting the coherent route for training youth and community workers in Wales. Previously employed as a youth worker and community education officer, John now maintains his interest in youth work practice as Chairman of North Ely Expeditions.

Sangeeta Soni is a senior youth and community worker in a multi-cultural inner city area of Birmingham. She is actively involved in the development and management of projects with young people, as well as training and staff development initiatives for youth workers. She is particularly concerned about issues of service delivery to Birmingham's Asian and Arab communities.

Dave Stannard is a senior youth and community worker with Birmingham City Council based at the 610 Community Centre in Kingstanding. His previous experience includes teaching and social work (Intermediate Treatment). He is particularly interested in the Duke of Edinburgh Award, young men's work and youth work through sports.

Neal Terry qualified in youth and community studies at Sunderland University and has worked for 12 years in a variety of voluntary sector youth work settings. He is currently Bishops Adviser in Youth Work for the Anglican Diocese of Newcastle, and studying Applied Theology at the University of Newcastle-upon-Tyne.

Joy Scott Thompson is an African-Caribbean woman born and raised in Handsworth, Birmingham. She started work as a volunteer and progressed to becoming a qualified youth and community worker. She is currently involved in training and development and youth work at her local church. She is married with a seven year old son, Tao.

Myra Topper is a qualified youth and community worker with 15 years professional experience and extensive previous experience as a volunteer. She has worked in a variety of settings with young Jewish people, and is currently Youth Services Manager for a large Jewish social services agency. Her interests include work with young women, and enabling young Jewish people to make their heritage relevant to their daily lives.

Other workers and young people contributing to the book

Imran Ali	Andrew Duncan	Shahid Sultan
Lisa Allen	Jeremy Fishman	Courtney Taylor
Mohinder Bagry	Bushra Habib	Ricki Vigon
Neil Bevan	Paul Jennings	Jamie Weinrich
Hannah Buddle	Shamsi Rashid	
Daniel Carmel-Brown	Meurig Roberts	

Introduction

They say that fortune favours the brave. Actually, a little good fortune is exactly what the youth service could do with at this point in time. But, in order to grasp it, I suspect we will need not only to be courageous but also confident and assertive. In other words, we will need to be both brave and bold. Still, such a stance is long overdue. Too much of the past twenty-five years has been spent agonising over the rights and wrongs of youth work's involvement in youth opportunities/training programmes, intermediate treatment, crime prevention, health promotion... and now...work with so-called 'disaffected' and socially excluded young people.

That is not to say that such issues are unimportant. After all everyone, including young people, is concerned about crime, adequate employment, meaningful education and social involvement. The question is, what is the youth work contribution? Admittedly, crime prevention may be an outcome of youth work. Young people may even decide to return to school or change their lifestyle as a result of their involvement in youth work. But this is a kind of side effect. It is not the main purpose of the work and those who maintain that youth workers can deliberately stop young people from stealing cars, taking drugs, getting pregnant, truanting from school, and all the rest of it are, quite frankly, unrealistically optimistic. Youth workers cannot be relied on to control young people nor to coerce or even win their acquiescence to the social and political status quo. And neither should they, since youth work is first and foremost concerned with young people's education not their subordination, indoctrination or indeed, recreation.

Education is the business of youth work. Enabling and supporting young people, at a critical moment in their lives, to learn and develop the capacities to reflect, to reason and to act as social beings in the social world. Not in any way they choose, but in accordance with the state of 'good faith' to which all human beings aspire. That state of living a life true to oneself. That, you may say, is a long way from harm minimalisation, condom distribution and homework clubs. Well, yes it is, and no it isn't. The important thing is not to mistake the finger pointing at the moon to be the moon itself. For such initiatives, like camping and canoeing, are a part of youth work in the sense that they point in that direction, but they are not youth work itself.

This assertion is, of course, not new. As long ago as 1948, L. J. Barnes commented that the 'prime endeavour' of the youth worker is to facilitate 'spontaneous behaviour' – not 'impulsive or capricious' but...

> *Our conception is [rather] of behaviour which is whole-hearted and whole-natured, as proceeding from a personality not divided against itself and not disorganised by feelings of guilt, inferiority, isolation or fear.* (Barnes 1948:30)

So it's not so much a case of back to the future, but forward to the past – a return to first principles. A return to the concept of youth work as educative and developmental, not because young people are 'in trouble' or 'cause trouble' but because they are young people in the process of creating themselves and the meanings which underpin their 'being' and guide their actions in the world.

This book is therefore about the concept of youth work, its **nature**, its philosophy and practice.

Philosophy

The starting point of this book is that the 'uniqueness' of youth work is to be found not in its methods, curriculum content or 'target groups', but in its **purpose**. And therefore that the future of youth work (and the youth service) rests not on its ability to achieve the objectives of other agencies, but on the clear articulation of the 'core' purpose of youth work – its underlying philosophy and potential outcomes.

My fundamental assertion is that youth work is an exercise in moral philosophy in the sense that it enables and supports young people to ask and answer the central questions of self – 'what sort of person am I?', 'what kind of relationships do I want to have with myself and others?', and 'what kind of society do I want to live in?'

Integral to this process is the issue of identity, 'who am I?' – a concept which refers not only to a person's **self-image** – their description of self, or knowledge of membership of a social group, but also to their **self-esteem** – an individual's evaluation of self; or the value and emotional significance attached to membership of particular social groups (Coleman and Hendry 1990:46).

This, of course, is not new to youth work. The development of self-image and, particularly, self-esteem have for long underpinned youth workers' explanation of their work and their practice. As such, there are numerous accounts of youth work initiatives which seek to extend young people's sense of achievement, reinforce their feelings of self worth and encourage them to take responsibility. In fact, such developments represent three of the dimensions which 'self theorists' have cast at the top of the hierarchy of dimensions of 'global self-esteem', namely:

1. Competence, or success in meeting achievement demands.
2. Social acceptance or attention, worthiness, and positive reinforcement received from significant others.
3. Control, or feelings of internal responsibility for outcomes.
   (Coleman and Hendry 1990:54).

However, there is a fourth dimension of 'global self-esteem' which, for the most part and for reasons of history, has received little attention in recent years. That is:

4. Virtue, or adherence to moral and ethical standards.
   (Coleman and Hendry 1990:54)

But even this is not strictly true since work around equal opportunities, identity-specific work (for example, with young women, young Black people, young lesbians and gay men) and, more broadly, anti-oppressive practice, have all sought to illuminate and challenge the oppressive structures and forces (both external and internal) which act to limit and constrain people's, and particularly young people's, lives. Inevitably, such work has involved the exploration of:

• values – what is believed to be right or wrong; good or bad
• virtue – acting in accordance with one's values.

Yet despite the significant impact of this work there is even now a tendency to view it either as a kind of aside – 'issue based' work with particular groups of young people; or as an aspect of methodology in terms of:

• promoting equality of access and opportunity to youth work
• 'doing' youth work in an anti-discriminatory or anti-oppressive way.

The effect of both these perspectives is to separate 'youth work' from the exploration of values as if 'youth work' is one thing and the exploration of values another. This, however, is a false separation. For if youth work seeks to support young people's understanding of themselves and the world, or their 'transition to responsible adulthood' (NYA 1997a), or even their 'growth through dependence to interdependence' (NYA 1999), then this necessarily involves young people in exploring their 'sense of self'. In other words, exploring their identity (self-image and self-esteem) which, in turn, involves working not only on matters relating to achievement, self worth and responsibility but also, and importantly, on the central issue of values and virtue.

In fact, the question of values and virtue is pivotal to the entire process since a person is, in effect, his or her values. That is to say, a person's sense of self is based, ultimately, on what they believe to be right or wrong/good or bad; and how they behave in relation to those beliefs. In other words, my self-image, sense of achievement, self worth and responsibility are all determined by what I believe to be good or bad, right or wrong. My values, therefore, underpin all that 'I am'. If I stop believing what I believe and, as a result, change the way I behave then I will no longer be the person I was. When I change my values, I change myself.

Exploring values is, therefore, not a part of youth work. It is all of youth work. It is the very foundation of the work and this is what makes youth work an exercise in moral philosophy. Because youth work is a process through which young people come to increasingly understand their values and integrate those values with their sense of identity and their actions in the world.

This is, of course, completely different from seeking to inculcate **particular** values in young people. What is being described here is a **process**. The process of moral philosophising through which young people gain the skills and dispositions needed to deliberate about what is 'good', not only for themselves in particular respects, but in terms of what is conducive to the 'good life' generally. The ability which Aristotle called the development of practical wisdom.

The process of moral philosophising is, therefore, an end in itself. Not a side effect or 'added value' but the very fabric of youth work. As such, it represents the essential foundation on which the observable approaches to youth work are built - approaches which recognise the constantly changing social and political context in which young people live, the experiences they share with others and the individual circumstances, needs, interests and aspirations they have as unique human beings.

But how can youth work practice achieve such noble ends?

Practice

Ask any youth worker about what youth workers **do** and they will tell you about two things – their **relationship** with young people and the youth work **process**. Both of which are not only elusive, but also tend to be regarded, by those outside of the work, as something of a hollow cry. Nonetheless, their constancy as a major theme within the work serves to strengthen the argument since, as Kleinig remarks, moral education is:

> *a matter of becoming a certain kind of person - of coming to care in certain kinds of ways and this is not directly achievable by means of syllabi and classroom techniques of the familiar*

kind. As much as anything, the development of virtue is a function of the relationships within which people move, and which provide a context for whatever moral reflection they engage in. (Kleinig 1982:253)

Youth workers are right. Relationships are the backbone of effective youth work practice. But what kind of relationships?

Relationships that are voluntary since a person cannot be coerced into engaging in moral philosophy; and relationships which:

- accept and value young people
- involve honesty, trust, respect and reciprocity

Relationships within which youth workers show concern and empathy for young people and where they take account of young people's experiences, opinions and ideas. The kind of relationship described by the McNair Committee, as long ago as 1944, (HMSO 1944:103) as being 'a guide, philosopher and friend' to young people and which I recently elaborated as providing:

> *a steer for young people through the philosophical enquiry into the nature, significance and inter-relationship of their values and beliefs, based on a relationship of true friendship – (following Aristotle's definition of) – wanting for someone what one thinks good for their sake and not for one's own* (Young 1999:82).

The important point is that 'philosophical enquiry' is a **process**. So youth workers are right again when they stress the central importance of relationships and processes which, in youth work terms, is the process of learning from experience. A process that develops, in young people, the critical skills of reflection, deliberation and rational judgement. A process that helps young people to develop the capacity to make sense of their experiences, themselves and their lives in the world.

The art of youth work

Yet, as is often the case, the simplest of things are also the most complex. For what is at once that simple act of 'friendship' is also the most profound of relationships. A relationship within which youth workers seek to engage with young people in the deliberate and purposeful process of experience, reflection and learning through which they gain the motivation and capacity to:

- examine their values;
- deliberate the principles of their own moral judgements; and
- develop the skills and dispositions to make informed decisions and choices that can be sustained through committed action.

It is this ability – the ability to make and sustain meaningful relationships within which young people engage in the process of moral philosophising – that I name the art of youth work.

But naming is not the same as invention. Youth work grounded in relationships and the reflective process has been going on for years. We just don't seem to talk about it much anymore.

Perhaps we are still running scared from the mid-nineteenth century when many clubs and youth organisations began to 'concern themselves overwhelmingly with the inculcation of intangible social and spiritual values amongst their clients rather than in improving their material well-being' (Jeffs 1979 quoted in Smith 1988:11). Perhaps we object to the strong tendency for education about values to end up meaning getting young people to accept and practice the values determined for them by someone else – be it the School Curriculum Assessment Authority (1996) or the Advisory Group on Citizenship (1998). Perhaps talking about relationships with ordinary young people is just not fashionable any more. The high-rollers are, after all, heavily into their needle exchanges and anti-pregnancy/anti-truancy programmes. Or perhaps the plain truth is that we are all just too busy dancing, since she who pays the piper calls the tune.

As for me, I take courage from the Albemarle Committee's comment that:

> The Youth Service should not seek to offer something packaged – 'a way of life', a 'set of values', 'a code of conduct' as though these were things which came ready-made, upon the asking, without being tested in living experience...If they feel the need young people must have the liberty to question cherished ideas, attitudes and standards and if necessary to reject them. (HMSO 1960:38)

Indeed, I am going one stage further by saying that youth work **should** encourage young people to question ideas, attitudes and standards - and not only their own but others' as well. That such questioning and critical reflection is, in fact, part of the essential purpose of youth work. I know that's a position not much in favour these days for, as Wainwright (1996) points out, there is a kind of taken-for-grantedness about contemporary ideology which encourages people to 'adapt to adverse conditions rather than seeking to challenge them' (1996: 78). No longer do we ask why so many young people are struggling with school. We set up 'alternative' provision and after-school clubs instead. No longer do we ask why so many (often very) young people are involved in drugs. We pursue harm minimalisation initiatives instead. That puts me with Wainwright when he suggests that our capacity to act as agents of social change is being eroded by the 'subordination of the critical consciousness' (1996:81). That same critical consciousness that enables us to take charge of ourselves and the meanings we compose for our lives.

So, in writing this book I went in search of youth workers who were prepared to talk with me about their philosophy and practice in making relationships with young people which engage them in philosophical enquiry – the raising of the critical consciousness. The result is a tapestry of approaches and contexts which illuminates the youth work relationship and process while setting it within the broader framework of the youth service's experience and history.

Of course, if youth work is to be preserved then it is not simply a matter of saying what it is and showing how we are currently doing it. It is also a matter of looking to the future. That means asking questions about the kind of skills needed by workers and, therefore, the kind of training needed to sustain such a vision of the work. My proposal here is that youth work training needs to provide workers with the opportunity for their own self-exploration, the examination of their own values, the development of their own critical skills and the enlargement of their own capacity for moral philosophy.

For, in the end, adapting Louden's observation about teachers (quoted in Cortazzi 1993:5) – youth workers do not merely deliver youth work. They define it, interpret it and develop it. It is what youth workers think, what youth workers believe and what youth workers do in practice that ultimately shapes the kind of experience and learning that young people get.

And when we are clear enough to be coherent and articulate about the 'core' purpose of youth work; and when we are brave enough to no longer rely on subterfuge; and when we are bold enough to assert the value of youth work for its own sake, then, and only then, will the youth service be equipped to confront the shifting sand and rising tide of the changing social and political agenda.

Part one
Philosophy

Philosophy is about understanding the **nature** of things. In this instance, the **nature** of youth work. For, while we are continually offered examples of youth work in terms of methods (detached work, groupwork, peer education), activities (outdoor pursuits, arts, sport), roles (befriender, advocate, counsellor) or issues (homelessness, unemployment, drugs, crime, sex), it is rarely the case that we consider the **common qualities** that enable all such examples to be known collectively as 'youth work'. That is, as a distinct activity in its own right; and one able to be distinguished from other forms of work with young people.

Sure, youth work literature is littered with references to social and informal education. But what does this mean? Particularly when police officers organise activities with young people, social workers and probation officers facilitate discussion groups, teachers engage in personal and social education, health workers do sex and drugs education, careers officers offer life skills training – and any of these may run specific groups for young women or talk with young people about unemployment or homelessness or crime. In fact, how can we talk about 'youth work' at all when just about everyone is laying claim to some kind of informal education which supports young people's personal development and informed decision making? (Young 1998).

Even the 1990s mass conversion to the principles of education, participation, empowerment and equality of opportunity, generated from the second Ministerial Conference (NYB 1991), cannot suffice to confirm youth work's 'uniqueness' since youth work does not own the monopoly on such principles. 'Equal opportunities' is, and has been for some time, part of the common parlance. And empowerment (with its prerequisite, participation), being the buzzword of the 1990s, belongs to everyone.

More important, though, is the fact that describing youth work in terms of its underpinning principles, methods and activities reveals little about **what it is** (its nature) or the reason for which it is done (its purpose). This is crucial, since the particular contribution that youth work makes to young people's lives cannot be understood by reference to methods, 'target groups' or 'curriculum'. Youth work's 'uniqueness' can only be demonstrated through an understanding of its **nature** and **purpose**.

Nature and purpose

Concern about the development of young people's values and the 'sort of people' they are to become is, and always has been, a fundamental feature of youth work thinking and practice. However, while early pioneers were often likely to conceive this in terms of the inculcation of particular values in young people, an examination of youth service reports and relevant texts reveals the path of changing interpretations. Changes which focus increasingly on the importance of young people being able to question ideas, attitudes, values and behaviour. Nonetheless, there is a consistent theme which has persisted from the late Victorian period to the present day. A theme which reveals that the **nature** of youth work is essentially concerned with young people's values and the development of moral and ethical standards – from obedience to anti-racism.

The reason for which youth work is done, its purpose, can also be traced via a review of relevant reports and texts. Interestingly, what one discovers is not the disparity over time or among voluntary youth organisations or local authority youth services, but the remarkable consistency of the youth service's concern for the personal and social development of young people.

The assertion here is twofold.

Firstly, despite the fact that young people's 'personal and social development' encompasses the various aspects of emotional, mental, physical and spiritual growth, at its heart lies the question of identity. This is because youth workers deliberately engage with people at a particular point in their lives. A period typically known as adolescence, which we have for long acknowledged as a time of 'increased emotional awareness and spiritual or idealistic development' (Macalister Brew, 1957:18); and a time for 'exploring the boundaries of freedom', examining 'how one sees oneself and is seen by others' and reflecting on 'personal identity' (Leighton, 1972:54). The intention here is not to cast young people's identity development as somehow problematic but rather to acknowledge that 'youth' has implications for youth work; and that central to 'youth' is the issue of identity.

Secondly, the questions of identity; 'what sort of person am I?' and 'what sort of person am I going to be?' (Davies and Gibson 1967:51) are inextricably bound to the question of values; 'what do I believe to be right or wrong/good or bad?'

And specifically in relation to self-esteem, the importance of virtue or adherence to moral and ethical standards (Coleman and Hendry 1990:54).

Therefore, if the purpose of youth work is to support the personal and social development of young people at that particular moment in their lives, then this necessarily and fundamentally involves consideration of:

- the concept and condition of 'youth'
- identity – in terms of the development of self-image and self-esteem
- values and the development of virtue – not only because this, in itself, reflects a major theme throughout the development of youth work but also because it is a principal dimension of 'global self-esteem' (Coleman and Hendry 1990:54).

Then and now

In one of Plato's dialogues, *Laches*, Socrates asks Laches the question "what is courage?". Laches' response is immediate – a man who does not run away in battle. However, as Socrates has no difficulty in demonstrating, Laches' answer is not a definition of courage, in general, but a particular example of courage. Socrates then asks "What is that common quality, which is the same in all cases, and which is called courage?" (Plato 1970:117). In other words, Socrates is asking "what is the **nature** of courage?"

I am asking the same question of youth work. "What is the **nature** of youth work? What is that common quality, which is the same in all cases, and which is called youth work?"

In seeking to answer this question I consulted, as a primary source, the major youth service reports. One of the reasons for doing this is because the reports are containable. After all, so much has been written. But more importantly, these reports considered submissions from both voluntary youth organisations and local authority services. They therefore effectively reflected the practice, perspectives and concerns of both sectors.

Also, one of the main problems of trying to identify the 'common quality' of youth work is the underlying problem of definition itself. That is, being able to decide what **is** and what **is not** 'youth work. A task made more difficult by the service's tendency for continuous metamorphosis, especially in matters of funding. My solution is to accept, as a benchmark, what these 'official' reports said youth work **ought** to be.

Finally, my primary interest concerns 'nature and purpose', the examination of which is, essentially, a philosophical exercise. This means pursuing what has actually been written about nature and purpose as opposed to the myriad of interpretations about the possible social, economic or political intentions which may lie behind different expressions of the work. Of course, these are important perspectives about which much has already been written and which, in terms of context and history, obviously impact on notions of purpose. Nonetheless, the exercise being undertaken here is unashamedly philosophical. I do so in the confidence that there are others more motivated and better qualified than I to undertake the sociological and political analyses which contribute to our greater understanding.

In addition, whilst the context of youth work and youth service policy statements are different across England, Wales and Northern Ireland (Becksy and Perrett 1999), much of the sentiment actually remains the same. Indeed, the inclusion here of the experiences and perspectives of workers from Wales and Northern Ireland, as well as England, acts to illustrate the commonality not only in provision and practice but also in purpose and values.

Then

As long ago as 1844, the YMCA adopted the following statement:

> The Young Men's Christian Association seeks to unite those young men who, regarding Jesus Christ as the God and Saviour, according to the Holy Scriptures, desire to be his disciples in their faith and in their life, and to associate their efforts for the extension of his kingdom amongst young men. (YMCA, 1987)

Similarly, in its establishment in 1883, the Boys' Brigade declared its object as:

> The advancement of Christ Kingdom amongst boys and the promotion of habits of obedience, reverence, discipline, self-respect and all that tends towards true Christian manliness.

So, while much of the early work (particularly with boys) was framed in clearly religious, and often militaristic, terms, it nonetheless made clear the 'sort of people' it hoped would develop. That is, people who exhibited the qualities of obedience, discipline and punctuality; people who participated in public service and had a clear religious commitment. (Davies and Gibson 1967; Eggleston 1976; Booton 1985; Smith 1988).

This clarity persists to the present day within the traditional voluntary sector with, for example, both the Scout and Guide Associations requiring members to pledge allegiance to the Scout/Guide Law which explicitly identifies the 'sort of person' a Scout or Guide is meant to be.

The Guide Law:
A guide is honest, reliable and can be trusted.
A guide is helpful and uses time and abilities wisely.
A guide faces challenge and learns from her experiences.
A guide is a good friend and a sister to all guides.
A guide is polite and considerate.
A guide respects all living things and takes care of the world around her.

Youth work in the maintained sector tended to define itself in more intangible ways. For example, in terms of the 'social and physical development of boys and girls' and the development of their 'body, mind and spirit' (Board of Education 1939). Or, alternatively, 'to develop the whole personality of individual boys and girls to enable them to take their place as full members of a free community.' (Board of Education 1940). Nonetheless, even such comments contained implicit statements about the 'sort of people' or 'personalities' that youth work should seek to 'produce'.

However, by 1945, the Youth Advisory Council was proclaiming that 'whatever the activity, and whatever the precise motive, the lessons to be learned are the same; co-operation, tolerance, free decision and joint responsibility' (Ministry of Education 1945) clearly identifying the values underpinning the work and those to be encouraged in young people.

Indeed, this broad theme of co-operation, free decision making and responsibility has persisted through the years with Sir John Redcliffe Maud referring to the need for young people to 'better equip themselves to live the life of mature, creative and responsible members of a free society'. (King George's Jubilee Trust 1951:13); and the Albemarle Committee reaffirming the importance of a 'sense of fellowship, of mutual respect and tolerance' (HMSO 1960:para 135), 'responsible personal choice' (para 351) and the capacity for 'making sound judgements' (para 136).

The Albemarle Report also suggested that the youth service should provide young people with challenging opportunities for them to 'display and to respect forms of pre-eminence in fields other than the academic' (para 137) – in other words to 'satisfy the sense of achievement for which all hunger' (para 210).

In 1969, *Youth and Community Work in the 70s* commented that:

> The primary goal of youth work is the social education of young people. Such a definition is not unimportant since, as we have seen, the aim changes as society changes. We are not so much concerned today as in the past with basic education, or with economic needs, or with the communication of an agreed belief or value system; but we are concerned to help young people to create their place in a changing society and it is their critical involvement in their community which is the goal. (HMSO 1969: para 152)

The report was mindful of the 'thin line which divides political education from political indoctrination' and, while appreciating the reasons for 'the little political education for young people in this country', nonetheless lamented the exclusion 'from the educational process and from discussions across the generation's many moral issues'. As a result, the report suggested that young people should engage in political education since:

> *Politics is concerned with life and how people live together. We see the new service providing many opportunities for young people to discuss matters of controversy and to share in the formation of public opinion.* (HMSO 1969: para 211)

The report also inspired renewed enthusiasm for young people's 'participation', the self-government of provision and the establishment of youth councils. The report's aspiration was the engagement of young people in a 'participant democracy'. In other words, 'an active society in which all are encouraged and enabled to find the public expression of their values, avoiding the extremes of indifference and alienation' (HMSO 1969: para 161).

The Albemarle Report's sanctioning of young people's right to 'question cherished ideas, attitudes and standards and, if necessary, to reject them' (HMSO 1960:38), therefore, consolidated a departure from the inculcation of particular values and preferred conduct, to a more questioning and critical stance for youth work and young people. A stance which gave prominence to young people engaging in discussions about moral issues and finding public expression of their values.

Experience and Participation (HMSO 1982) proclaimed 'virtual unanimity' amongst those consulted by the Review Group that:

> *the fundamental purpose of the youth service is to provide programmes of personal development comprising, in shorthand terms, social and political education... The twin aims of this purpose are thus affirmation and involvement – affirming an individual in their proper identity and involving an individual in relationships with other individuals and institutions.*
> (HMSO 1982: para 7.3)

The **experience** to which the report's title referred was the experience of: being valued and accepted as a person; measuring oneself against others; making choices and seeing them through; enduring and living with hard reality; playing a part in a common enterprise; being responsible to and for others; receiving, giving and sharing ideas; and perceiving others' needs. (HMSO 1982: para 3.5)

In relation to **participation**, the Review Group commented:

> *...the primary purpose of participation in the youth service is to give the young individual a sense of belonging, a sense of identity, and the skills, confidence and assurance needed to participate not only in his club or organisation but also in society at large.* (HMSO 1982: para 5.17)

This put youth work squarely, and explicitly, back in the territory of identity formation – with attention to young people's self-image and self-esteem. However, *Experience and Participation* also emphasised another important aspect of the work. That was the social, economic and political contexts in which young people live their lives; and the powerful impact of these on their personal development. Specifically, it commented on the damaging effects of racism, sexism and attitudes towards people with disabilities (HMSO 1982). This acted not only to affirm existing and emerging practice but also established the legitimacy of discussing cultural and societal as well as personal values.

In fact, following the publication of *The Thompson Report* (HMSO 1982), many local youth services conducted reviews which resulted, inevitably, in policy changes and the formulation of new statements of purpose. While the primary aims of many services were often conceived in 'individual' terms, alongside this were two further strands of emerging youth service aims.

> First, and this has been developing over a number of years, is an increasing recognition by the Service of the social and political context within which young people live. This recognition generally takes the form of explicitly acknowledging some of the major structural divisions in British society, especially those of class, gender and race, which help determine young people's views and concerns and which materially affect their social and political circumstances. (Smith 1987:19)

The second strand focused on the role of the service as an advocate with and for young people – 'the movement towards recognising young people's interests and viewing the work of the service in relation to young people in a collective sense...' (Smith 1987:20).

Against this backdrop, and the surge in developments in practice, the second Ministerial Conference for the Youth Service recommended that:

> The purpose of youth work is to redress all forms of inequality and to ensure equality of opportunity for all young people to fulfil their potential as empowered individuals and members of groups and communities and to support young people during the transition to adulthood. (Statement of Purpose NYB, 1991:16)

It also stated that youth work offers young people opportunities which are:

- **educative** – *enabling young people to gain the skills, knowledge and attitudes needed to identify, advocate and pursue their rights and responsibilities as individuals and as members of groups and communities locally, nationally and internationally;*
- **designed to promote equality of opportunity**
  - *through the challenging of oppressions such as racism and sexism and all those which spring from differences of culture, race, language, sexual identity, gender, disability, age, religion and class; and*
  - *through the celebration of the diversity and strengths which arise from those differences.*

- participative – *through a voluntary relationship with young people in which young people are partners in the learning process and decision making structures which affect their own and other young people's lives and their environment.*
- empowering – *supporting young people to understand and act on the personal, social and political issues which affect their lives, the lives of others and the communities of which they are a part.* (NYB, 1991:16)

The effect on practice

Nonetheless, despite the changing emphasis over the past 160 years, much of the underpinning ideas about the nature and purpose of youth work can still be found in current practice.

For example, in terms of the commitment to young people's emotional, mental, physical and spiritual growth:

> We have the stated aims about emotional, mental, physical and spiritual growth. So we're not specifically interested in someone's academic ability. In terms of the physical, some people would say that we don't do that very well, whereas others see camping as a physical activity. Certainly, we're not as sporty as we used to be and there are a lot of people who regret that. So right now there's a move to think some more about sport but not competitive sport necessarily – things like girl's football where they're developing the skills with a ball rather than having to get into a league. What we're trying to do is give a balance so you get your outdoors and your arts in Guiding. You don't have to choose between one or the other.
>
> In terms of the emotional, some of that's about being with other people and being in control of thinking about the effect on others of what you've said or done. Learning about relationships. There are a lot of Ranger Units now that are getting into things like sessions with Relate focused on taking control of a relationship, deciding what you're looking for in a relationship, not being put upon and issues like that. I think that's probably a response to the teenage pregnancy issue.
>
> The spiritual dimension is quite difficult in Guiding because, for some people, this is very much linked to the church. And, in fact, some units are clearly linked to a church or, for reasons of cost, use church premises. But spirituality is not just about religion. It's something to do with a connection with nature – going to the mountains and feeling a part of the world. Sleeping under the stars. Just being in the environment and remembering that you are only human. It can be really simple. For example, we had a young woman with a disability in our unit and then one day we were all sitting on the grass and we realised that she'd never sat on the grass. She wanted to join us so we helped her out of her wheelchair and she was completely stunned. She just couldn't believe it.

The 'responsible personal choice' and 'sense of achievement' to which the Albemarle Report referred:

I'm into creating opportunities for young people to succeed, experience a sense of achievement and grow in self-esteem. That's how I see youth work. Increasing young people's expectations of life and raising their horizons.

We have a vested interest in developing young people who are able to reflect on their experience, consider different courses of action and the effect on other people, make choices, who have the confidence to bring about change or influence their lives and who hopefully will not do that at the expense of other people but with other people.

The self-government, sense of community and young people's understanding of their 'place in a changing society' underlined by *Youth and Community Work in the 70s*:

Self-government ranges from being able to choose what your Guide unit is going to do – probably from a prescribed list – say choose four activities from a list of eight or something like that; through to a Ranger unit that sets it's own constitution and programmes and works it out for itself – writes it's own letters, booking speakers and venues, organising the mini-bus, sorting out the catering arrangements. Just doing everything.

Youth work is about enabling young people to find themselves. It's about them being able to look at where they're at in their lives, the way they interact with other people and feeling that they can make an impact on others around them. Maybe this is really simplistic but I feel if I can make an impact on, say, three young people during their lifetime which means that they take on some of the values about how people treat each other and offer that to the people they come into contact with then you'd have a kind of domino effect. And that could actually create a sense of community, a connection, a sense of being a human being that is far bigger than just you or me.

What I've always tried to do in my work with young people is to help them explore where they are at in their life, their relationships and how they see themselves within society – their position, their schooling, what they do when they come along to the club, how they interact with each other, what their demands are, what their requests are, how they feel, how they want to be treated as young people. But in order to work effectively with young people with disabilities you also have to take into consideration a lot of the external influences. More so, I think, than in mainstream youth work. So I have to think about parental wishes and influences. Particularly when you are talking about personal relationships, sexual relationships and what that actually means, but this is not to say the young people's wishes are ignored.

The Thompson Report's emphasis on the 'experience' of being valued, identity and the value base of the work:

Youth work is about enabling young people to think about themselves and their life. Who they are as human beings and what their contribution is and can be to society. It's about giving them positive strokes and letting them know that they exist and are valuable human beings. That's regardless of what they've experienced and where they've come from. It's just seeing them as they come through the door, respecting them and not judging them.

We see our main purpose as seeking to influence young people's levels of self-esteem, motivation and confidence. That means helping them to manage their anger and frustration and increase their ability to effect meaningful changes in their lives.

Youth work is based on a value base that says 'I will not judge or criticise you simply because you are young or black, or poor, or gay or lesbian but there are things that I will challenge you about.' So that's about giving people an opportunity to recognise their responsibility and their role in their own life. And what they need to do is to be able to demonstrate, through a process that allows them to gather information, the ability to base their life decisions on that information.

The Ministerial Conferences' commitment to empowerment, participation and equality of opportunity:

Youth work is about empowerment – supporting young people to increase their confidence in expressing themselves, their needs, their desires, their fulfilments. It's about them being able to communicate with other people and make constructive decisions while taking into account the different options available and the possible consequences.

Education, capacity building, empowerment and equality of opportunity are all part of a community development approach that starts where young people are at, is dictated by their needs, goes at their pace, and is flexible to fit different situations. Even though this may look casual to the outsider, or even the young people, it represents very deliberate interventions by the youth worker.

Now

In 1997 a working group serviced by the National Youth Agency produced a *Youth Service Statement of Purpose* which stated that:

Youth work supports young people in their transition from childhood to responsible adulthood, encourages their social development and individual fulfilment and helps them to engage fully in society. (NYA 1997a)

The statement confirmed its commitment to equal opportunity and young people's contribution as partners in the learning process. It affirmed the service's commitment to young people's voluntary participation and the encouragement of their critical and creative responses to their world. (NYA 1997a)

Most recently, the statement of key purpose contained in the draft *National Occupational Standards for Youth Work* referred to encouraging young people's 'personal and social education and helping them to take a positive role in the development of their communities and society.' (NYA 1999)

The last few years have therefore witnessed a withdrawal from the more overtly political or collective perspective of the Ministerial Conference statement to a more individual emphasis on young people's personal development, individual fulfilment and social involvement.

At the same time, the youth service has excelled in laying claim to its contribution to addressing urgent social issues (United Kingdom Youth Work Alliance 1996) and promoting possible roles for youth workers in preparing young people for work, reducing youth crime and anti-social behaviour, promoting healthy living and other such initiatives. (NYA 1998). But this, of course, is not new.

> *The problem that we face, and we've often done very badly at this, is actually being able to describe accurately what we are trying to do. I think we've been very chameleon like, particularly in Wales, in terms of trying to be everything depending on who has the money and what those with the money are saying about what it is we need to do. We had those little forays into YOPs and Intermediate Treatment and now we have this debate around New Deal. So we don't describe what we do very well and it's also difficult to quantify it. But I actually believe that the youth service, if it is able to describe it's work well, is also able to provide both hard and soft evidence about it's effect on crime reduction, health promotion, citizenship and a range of government or funding body initiatives. That we can do all of those things. But that's not because those are the things that we set out to do. It's because those are the things that we achieve by being effective youth workers.*

So, whilst crime prevention, health promotion, etc. may be outcomes of youth work, they are not central to its aim. Indeed, the urgent social issues of the day are problems of 'political making and economic change' (Bloxham 1997:1). Working with young people cannot 'cure' these problems because young people did not make them. They inherited them. Therefore:

> *trying to solve complex social problems such as juvenile crime, very young mothers or drug abuse through poorly funded youth work, as we have done in recent years, is [also] destined to flounder.* (Bloxham 1997:13)

Young people's views

Notwithstanding, young people themselves are often very clear about the nature and purpose of youth work.

> *Youth work isn't a job. You can't look at it like it's just a job unless you are in it for the wrong reasons. Like if you were just out to get a job and you go into youth work you won't really enjoy it. To be a youth worker you have to want to encourage young people's development*

– no matter who they are. They help your development socially and with your confidence. They encourage you to do activities, go out and meet people. You start doing things that you don't normally do. They make you talk and you can talk about anything really. They're there to have fun with you and look out for you and at the same time help you to discover all the aspects of life that you may not discover by yourself. Like before I got into youth work I just stayed in at week-ends. I didn't do anything. But now we go out, sometimes we do fund raising events and all sorts of things. I would never have dreamed of doing some of the stuff we've done like face painting and handing out flyers because I was really self-conscious. But I did it and it was a big thing for me. We also did a parachute jump which was quite good. The group I'm in now we just think of as many bizarre things as we can and just do them because we're never going to get a chance again.

The role of the youth worker is to help young people build their confidence and realise that they are needed and valued and that they can do loads of super things – helping them to respect others and have a community feeling. It's about making them feel like they may be different but there's still a right track that you should be on as a person. So the youth worker helps you to find that right track because they see what you are capable of. But you choose that track as a young person because they can't force you to do anything. If I'd never met…(the worker) I wouldn't be so headstrong about the right thing. I would have been headstrong about the wrong thing. But now I see the importance of things like the work ethic, respecting others, appreciating your culture and just not being nasty and realising that the world doesn't revolve around you. But I think you realise that. That's just a teenage thing. But sometimes I know that people carry it on.

I've got friends at school but when I came here I met a lot of new friends and, by getting into arguments with them, it helped me to realise what I was doing wrong and stuff like that and that has helped me to change – because when you get into arguments with people and then you think did I really do that and if I did then I think well I'm going to change it and gradually you get better. I'd like people to say I'm a nice person – understanding, caring, a good listener.

I've learnt about what sort of person I am through meeting different people every day. I think you also learn about what sort of person you want to be when you are older. Like role models in a sense that help you to become more self aware about who you are and where you fit into all of this. And then you start thinking. Because when you're at school you're just confined to school. Come home, do your homework, have an argument with your parents. Next morning you get up, have your breakfast and go to school again. But being with youth workers it's completely different. Since I've known them I've become less negative. I feel like I have something to offer now.

I've developed an awful lot as a person in the four years that I've been coming here. I think if I hadn't have come here I would never have learnt what I've learnt about how to treat people in a better way and how people react to different situations. I've become more considerate and more caring and I understand a lot more about different people and their different backgrounds and experiences. I've also learnt that there is a lot more I could do because although I have some good qualities, like being reliable and trustworthy, there are also some bad qualities that I have. In time I need to develop those bad aspects and improve on the good ones. What I'd really like is to be able to say 'What you see is what you get.' No false pretences about what I believe. No fake outside image. Just trying to be down-to-earth and natural. That's how I'd like people to see me.

Social, political and informal education

The problem for the youth service is that, despite its rich history and collective wisdom, it has often failed to express clearly, coherently and consistently the nature and purpose of youth work. The apparent lack of a coherent theory of practice to which some have pointed (Smith 1988; Paraskeva 1992) has been caused, therefore, not by the absence of clearly defined concepts and guiding principles, but by the service's inclination to accept that every initiative taken by organisations considered to be part of the 'youth service' could be named youth work. The result is that definitions of the work have sometimes been constructed not from the basis of purpose, but rather from a desire to reflect and affirm existing provision and practice. (NACYS 1989)

However, since its inception, three terms have continued to be reiterated in relation to purpose and practice in the youth service – social education, political education and, more recently with refreshed vigour, informal education. What is significant is that whilst these terms have been variously used, an examination of their 'definitions' reveals the enormous extent of common **meaning** and intention which exists. For example, the National Advisory Council for the Youth Service described the aim of 'social education' as:

> to enable persons as individuals and as members of their communities to take charge of their personal lives and play a responsible role in the life of the communities so that they may be able to make decisions for themselves and have a part in the decision making processes of the community. Youth work helps young people to become critically aware of themselves and others including the wider society, and to take steps to improve their situation. (NACYS, 1989: para 8)

Whereas The Thompson Report's discussion of 'political education' asserted that:

> politics is the term we apply to the forces which give society the shape and direction it has…These forces are based on attitudes – of individuals and of groups – and spring from the activity resulting from those attitudes – i.e. from people acting on their convictions. (para 5.34)…What

is required is experience of such a kind that the young people learn to claim their right to influence the society in which they live and to have a say in how it is run. It is active participation in some form of political activity, formal or informal, which really counts. (HMSO 1982: para 5.37)

More recently, the term 'informal education' has re-emerged, not as a description of provision and activities provided for young people 'out-of-class' (HMSO 1960: para 131), but to characterise a particular form of practice which has, at its heart, the idea of 'critical dialogue' (Smith 1988) or 'conversation' (Jeffs and Smith 1996).

However, in discussing the **purpose** of the work, Smith suggests that:

practitioners should set out to enable individuals to autonomously pursue their own well-being. In particular, they should seek to enlarge young people's understanding of their own well-being so that they may weigh their own needs with those of others, help them to display civic courage, and enable them to gain the knowledge, skills and disposition necessary to think and act politically. (Smith 1988:xii)

Smith's proposition is therefore that young people should be enabled to make free reasoned choices [autonomy] to pursue what is 'good' and supports human flourishing – theirs and others [well-being] even in the face of contrary opinion or opposition [civic courage] (1988:113).

Consistency and coherence

A review of the service's sense of purpose therefore reveals that, although expressed with different emphases, there is a clear consistency in the service's commitment to young people's:

- personal development – well-being of body, mind and spirit
- autonomous, free, informed decision making
- active participation
- critical involvement in their community and society

Central to this is:

- An understanding of equality which extends beyond ensuring equality of access and opportunity to recognising the social, economic and political context in which young people live their lives (HMSO 1982); and challenging oppressions based on differences in culture, race, language, sexual identity, gender, disability, age, religion and class. (NYB 1991)
- A commitment to supporting young people to question their own and others' ideas, attitudes, values and beliefs, share in the formation of public opinion, and claim their right to influence the society in which they live (i.e. act politically).

What becomes self-evident is not the differences in expression or language regarding the nature and purpose of youth work but the coherence in meaning and intention. Particularly in terms of enabling and supporting young people's capacity to take charge of themselves and their lives and participate in decision making processes and political activity in their community and society at large.

However, given that participation in decision making and political activity necesarily involves some 'vision of the good' then it is clear that the nature, or common quality of the work is, and always has been, a concern with young people's values and the development of moral and ethical standards.

Over the last ten years, most of my work has been a process of getting young people to explore alternative beliefs and value systems. When you are young you almost believe that this is how life will always be for you. So, in claiming the values of your peers, or school, or capitalism, you've not necessarily had the space to explore what you really believe. That opportunity has not been provided in schools because over the past ten years they have become very task and exam focused, which means that the possibility of exploring what's actually on the curriculum is no longer there in any real sense. There is personal and social education which does provide young people with some information – for example about drugs or contraception or HIV or whatever. But what it tends not to do is get young people to engage on a deeper level about how they actually think, feel and act given all of this information.

My mission isn't to make young people be something. My mission is to explore with young people their potential and the wealth of life options available to them. When you are young you don't necessarily feel you have any options apart from keeping up with your peer group. For instance, you may feel that you have to do something against your own values in order to get those trainers or engage in sexual practices before you were ready because there were pressures upon you. But if you've given young people a chance to consider not only their options but the possibility of choice, then it becomes clear that there is a range of value systems and you can choose any of them.

Youth work is about engaging with young people on an agenda that is about knowledge of the self and how young people perceive the world and their place within that world. So if we were organising a dance workshop we would ensure that the tutor we engage is aware of our agenda. Yes, they may be doing street dancing, hip-hop or whatever but what we want

cont...

conveyed to young people is an understanding of the link that that style of dance has with the long tradition of Black dance, whether that's from West Africa or the Harlem Renaissance. The important thing is to understand the continuity. Not that nothing is new but understanding that what they come with is a transformation of what already is. And that they are connected to a long line of people who have enabled them to exist in the way that they exist here today.

(Ella Jess)

'Youth'

The concept of 'youth' is central to the concept of 'youth work'. Not simply because youth work focuses its attention on a particular age range, but also because 'adolescence' is typically portrayed as involving various transitions, for example in relation to clarity about rights, roles and responsibilities. (Coleman, Catan and Dennison 1997). Specifically, within youth work, 'adolescence' is often perceived as a period of transition 'to adulthood' or, alternatively, the transition from 'dependence to independence or interdependence'.

When I think about it, I think the 'transition' idea is like going on a journey. When you go on a journey you need a guide, especially if it's a journey that you've never been on before and young people haven't been on this journey before. Now that guide may be a book or some sort of information or sometimes it's a person. As I unravel this, it seems to me that young people are on this journey where the difference is that the guide doesn't tell you what to do. The guide gives you information and sometimes advice. And you engage with the guide in a process that's about figuring out which way to go. Sometimes the road may take a turn you didn't expect and you may end up in a swamp. At which point the guide may have to rescue you and help you out – help you back onto your journey again. Actually it's a journey that we all travel. But as we get older we gain more experience that hopefully we learn from. One of the things we learn is that life has a lot of swamps. The trick is to see them coming and learn how to avoid them.

cont...

If young people are in transition then we have to be able to say when that journey ends. For me, being an adult means being able to make decisions and accept the consequences of those decisions. It is when you are clear about what you are and are not prepared to do in terms of what is acceptable to you as a person. It's about having a solid set of principles that you use to measure your actions.

(Kevin Crawford)

However, despite the emphasis on the 'personal journey', we also need to remember that 'adolescence' is a social phenomenon to be understood in relation to the social setting of the individual, the pressure of social expectations, and the relative influence of different agents of socialisation. (Coleman 1992:11) It is a social setting within which young people are 'neither a homogeneous group nor a static one'. (Jones quoted in Wyn and White 1997:8)

Notwithstanding, if adolescence is a period of 'transition to adulthood' then we must be able to identify when that transition ends. That is, we need to be able to define the concept of 'adulthood'. Kiernan (cited in Morrow and Richards 1996) defines adulthood as involving:

- finishing full-time education
- entry into the labour market
- leaving home
- the establishment of an independent household
- entry into marriage or cohabitation
- parenthood

Jones and Wallace (cited in Morrow and Richards 1996) also include the acquisition of full citizenship.

Morrow and Richards themselves classify 'the normative **ideal** of contemporary adult status into four main categories' – political or legal adulthood, financial or economic adulthood, social and sexual adulthood, parenthood (1996:10). They also assert that major changes in each of these aspects of transitions results in an overall disconnection and complex (rather than linear) series of 'transitions'.

For youth workers the questions of 'transition' and 'adulthood' are nowhere near as clear cut.

I don't think young people's transitional status is at all clear. It's not like leaving school at 16 and becoming an adult. Mass unemployment has completely changed that. Also, young people are developing their awareness of life at quite an early stage. They are very aware of sex and issues around sex. They are aware of a lot of things that I certainly wasn't aware of at their age. So I think the experience is just about moving on and learning and gaining experience. And I think that applies to adults as much as it does to young people because I don't see a clear demarcation between what young people know and their experience; and what older people know and their experience.

I think the idea that young people are in 'transition' is insulting. It gives the impression that young people are unfinished 'products' or 'work in progress' which can be shaped by whatever the adult population decides is 'in their best interest'. It does not confer the status of citizen on them which in turn does not see them as having a right to be involved in decision making.

Many young people assume very adult roles in life as parents, carers or workers. To continuously focus on the future in terms of their 'transition to adulthood' or independence or interdependence means that the present is not something to be savoured and enjoyed.

I'm not convinced about the category of adolescence or this idea that young people are in transition. Primarily it says to me that there is still a desire in some parts to label and thereby box young people into some easily definable category that can be easily dealt with. This is especially in relation to a personal value base. I don't think we should assume that the teenage years should be used as some impressionable age when we can deliver into their heads the pre-agreed terms of the current social contract. Nor should we assume that once we achieve adult status, however defined, our value base is intact and immutable.

It's very easy to say that young people with disabilities have the same rights as any other young person but in reality that is not the truth. There are all sorts of pressures from significant others and services that create situations whereby young people are not supported or allowed to exercise the independence that is usually associated with adulthood. That anxiety and fear and desire to both control and protect starts almost from the day that young person is born and so often has very little to do with the actual abilities, capabilities or capacity of the young person concerned.

For these workers, then, young people are not 'work in progress' in their 'transition to adulthood'. Their understanding is rather of an on-going experience within which young people's present (as opposed to future) lives should be seen as something of value, in itself, to be 'savoured and enjoyed'. In addition, there is concern that young people's 'transitional status' may lead to others deciding what is 'in their best interest' and thereby delivering them into the 'pre-agreed terms of the current social contract.' Intrinsic to that concern, is the desire for young people to be able to question the terms of the present 'social contract' and decide **for themselves** what serves their 'best interest'.

However, while it may be difficult to distinguish a clear 'demarcation between what young people know and their experience; and what older people know and their experience', it is not suggested that the experience of being a young person and that of being an adult is the same. The point is that young people's knowledge and experiences are not necessarily exclusive to them in the sense that what they may know about (e.g. sex), some adults may also know about; and what they may experience (e.g. unemployment), some adults may also experience. Nonetheless, the particular experience of being young is a biological reality. As Wyn and White point out:

> *Age is a concept which is assumed to refer to a biological reality. However, the meaning and the experience of age, and of the process of ageing, is subject to historical and cultural processes...whereby age is socially constructed, institutionalised and controlled in historically and culturally specific ways.* (Wyn and White 1997: 9–11)

Therefore, it is not the objective reality of age that is contested but rather the subjective 'meaning' with which 'youth' has been imbued. Specifically, the notion that adolescence represents a transitory period during which the young person seeks to attain some defined, fixed and immutable end state known as 'adulthood'.

For youth work, then, the focus is on young people at that particular moment in their lives when they are developing their awareness, seeking answers and, crucially, beginning to explore their beliefs, values and choices. This moment is not understood as the beginning of an end (i.e. transition to adulthood or independence or interdependence) but as the beginning of a lifelong process of reflection, learning and growth.

> *There is a moment in people's lives, call it adolescence, when they embark on a new and often painful journey. That moment is different from what they have experienced before and different from what they will experience in the future. In that moment they begin to crystallise their upbringing and the beliefs and values that make them who they are. They are asking questions and they are searching for answers.*

There is a moment of change then. A moment which may include some of the psychological transitions and sociological pressures discussed above. But youth workers do not understand this as a transition ending in some enduring existence where, as adults, young people will no longer experience 'status ambiguity'; where their rights, roles and responsibilities are clear (Coleman 1992); or where having a job, an independent household, marriage/cohabitation, parenthood and full citizenship will finally confirm their political, financial, social and sexual status as 'adults'. (Morrow and Richards 1996) Youth workers understand adolescence as the beginning of a reflective process within which:

> *The role of the youth worker is to recognise and nurture that process. We need to support young people to ask their questions and find their answers by enabling their reasoning and opening up their choices.*

Adolescence is therefore seen, by youth workers, as a moment of questioning – a moment in which young people reflect critically on their sense of self, their beliefs and values. It is a moment which demands attention to enabling 'reasoning' and the opening up of options. This is not to suggest that youth workers are completely devoid of any interest in the concept of adulthood, after all:

> *Youth is a relational concept because it exists and has meaning largely in relation to the concept of adulthood…it is problematic largely because adult status itself is problematic.* (Wyn and White 1997: 9-11)

From youth workers' perspectives:

> *Adulthood is when you take control of your own life. When you are responsible for your own actions. I recognise that there are some people who never do that – because of an inability or financial situation or whatever they may remain dependent on others. But for the majority of us I think you are an adult when you are in control of your life and responsible for your own actions. I used to think that was when you left home but in Guiding I've actually met a lot of women who choose to live at home for financial reasons but are definitely running their own life.*

> *Adulthood is a very individual thing but I think some of the common features would be people who are somehow at peace with themselves, having a sense of themselves and where their life is going, and a feeling of responsibility to themselves and others. The kind of self-respect that you get from feeling responsible for yourself and what you want to do with your life. It's a wonderful feeling. The thing is I'm 26 and I don't know if I feel like an adult sometimes. I know I am. Legally I am an adult. But I don't know if I always feel it.*

> *Adulthood is when you are able to make your own decisions and take control of what you want to do. Being able to say what you believe even if everyone else believes something different. Having enough personal confidence to be able to give to others. Being able to be in a group of your peers but be an individual. Accepting your responsibilities.*

> *To me, the adult state is about the ability to engage in a clear exchange of information and being non-manipulative in the sense that it's not about playing games or trying to outdo somebody else or make them feel bad. So, when we talk about adulthood as a state of independence, what I'm not clear about is whether we mean being financially independent, or living away from parents, or some other definition. I actually think there is another way*

of understanding independence, and that is in terms of the way a person conducts their life. The way that they acknowledge where they are at and their feelings. The existence of a clear value system. Having one's own thoughts and desires. For a young person with a disability, it may be that they will never be financially independent. Or will not necessarily have their own home. For some, they will always live in a system where there are carers or support workers. But that doesn't mean that they will also have an absence of a clear sense of self, independent thought and a worked out set of values. And in that sense, they have the potential to be as independent as the next person.

Adulthood means being in control of yourself. And the thing about being young is about feeling like 'I'm not in control of myself.' So you get this talk about pregnancy like it's this accident that happened. And I keep saying 'how can it be an accident?' You were there. He was there. You engaged in sexual intercourse. That's not accidental. An accident is when you trip and fall down the stairs. The conception may be something that you didn't think would happen to you but the whole thing isn't accidental because you got to a point where you could have made a decision. So adulthood is the capacity to make decisions and choices based on the knowledge of the consequences for yourself, community and ultimately all that is, not placing the responsibility for your actions elsewhere. So saying your hormones are running away with you or you're under stress or you can't control your anger is reneging on the choices you made and your responsibilities. Adulthood is about having emotional maturity; control over yourself including your emotions.

The qualities and capacities which these workers attribute to their concept of 'adulthood' therefore include:

- the ability to engage in a clear exchange of information without seeking to manipulate or 'outdo' others
- having self-respect and personal confidence
- taking responsibility for one's own actions
- making choices from an informed position having considered the consequences for yourself, the community and others
- being in control of your life and having a sense of where your life is going
- being able to be in a group of peers and still be an individual
- being able to say what you believe even if everyone else believes something different
- being able to give to others
- acknowledging where you are at – your feelings, thoughts and desires
- having emotional maturity and control of yourself including your emotions
- having a clear value system

Interestingly, these qualities are neither age specific nor do they reflect the kinds of qualities and conditions which Coleman (1992) and Morrow and Richards (1997), for example, identify as typifying the state of adulthood. There is no mention here of having achieved clarity regarding one's (social and political) rights, roles and responsibilities. No discussion of particular life events – e.g. leaving school, getting a job, leaving home, marriage, parenthood. No reference to the level of the political, legal, financial, social or sexual independence which adult status may be thought to confer.

Youth workers' understanding of 'adulthood' is in fact much more akin to Davies and Gibson's much earlier view of 'maturity' in the sense that it is:

> a highly developed sensitivity to the requirements of others on oneself and a flexibility to express the appropriate aspects of one's individuality to meet the situation. Such maturity does not come rapidly and assumes the self-discipline and humility which comes from a careful discernment of one's own social situation and personal potentiality. (Davies and Gibson 1967:94)

But again we have to be careful not to suggest that that particular moment of 'youth' does not bring with it its own pressures, questions and concerns. For, despite the difficulties we may have with defining the concepts of 'adolescence', 'adulthood' and indeed 'youth', we cannot deny that there is a specific experience, or range of experiences, resulting from being young in Britain today. A reality that young people are themselves only too aware of.

> Adolescence seems to kind of defeat the purpose of childhood. I got to 16 and realised that I didn't really know what a childhood was because I thought 'was that my childhood?' Up to that point I'd been sheltered by school and a whole system. Then I got to 16 and thought 'Oh'. I think it's good that schools treat you more like an adult in your last year. It kind of prepares you. But the truth is you don't really know what you're doing. You just think you'll go on the dole. You just look for another system that you can secure yourself with. I think parents have to play a big role in that. They have to give you some of the independence that you need to grasp and experience. The funny thing is, even though leaving school is a really big moment, it doesn't really hit you until you're not there and you're thinking 'I'd be in maths now' or 'I'd be getting told off now', 'I'd be wagging now'. It doesn't hit you until then how sheltered you've been. How lenient they were and how secure the whole environment was. You don't realise until you're out of it all. I left school at 16 and I'd gone through the whole of those 16 years with someone telling me what to do. I felt lost when I left school.
>
> I think youth workers have a really important role today – like in the late 1990s – because it's such a fast pace society. It's like the identity crisis. Who am I? There's all these people around me. Different cultures. Different languages. Different religions. And there's more and more pressures on young people that are increasing the rate of distress like with eating

disorders. But it isn't just about mental health. It's anything and everything to do with young people.

Nobody can judge what the next person can or cannot cope with. People are individual people. So for some people you won't even notice adolescence. But for others you will do. And what you see is that it's a time of confusion. It's an awful time because I'm going through it now and I'm asking myself all these questions like who am I, what is my role in society, where am I, where do I go, what is my status? And it's not just about who and what and where I am. It's about how you feel within yourself and how you feel about this glamour around you about being size ten. How do you feel about these ideals that you have to live up to? How do you feel about the fact that one day you're going to have to leave home and then your support just stops. And that's what contributes to distress within this society. Because you're moving away from the extended family and with new technology you are moving away all of the time and becoming more and more isolated.

Being a teenager is the worst part of your life – well so far anyway. There's so many things going round in your head and you're realising about people. Like when you're a child a smile is just a smile. But when you're older, when you're around your teenage years a smile is different. There's a malicious smile, a cheeky smile, a false smile, a genuine smile. All these things are entering into your head and that's just a smile and you've got four things already that you're not sure about. But it's just life. Everything. And for me being Asian in England is really hard. That was hard at school. It just seems like the world is really big. You don't realise how big it is. And there is so much hormones and emotion and all sorts of things that you don't know about and there's no answers for. It's terrible.

'Youth' and youth work

Of course, there are all sorts of young people since they are, after all, unique individuals who:

- Live in different circumstances – e.g. in relation to housing, personal relationships, educational experience, rural isolation or employment.
- Face different issues – e.g. in terms of health or crime.
- Have different interests – e.g. sport, music, the environment.
- Aspire to different achievements – e.g. in terms of their academic achievement, career choices or life goals.

Young people are also different because some of them are women and others are men. Some are black people, others white people. Some have a disability. Some identify as lesbian or gay. And they come from a range of class backgrounds and religious commitments. Faced with such diversity it may appear that young people are not really 'a group' at all, since their identification as a social group requires the existence of some shared experience or quality. One is therefore forced to asked 'what is the common experience that young people share?'. The answer to which is, of course, that 'being young' is the common experience that young people share.

But while different young people may experience the psychological changes of 'adolescence' in different ways and to varying degrees, one consistent experience shared by them is the imbalance of power between young people and adults which means that, despite wanting to be shown respect, young people often feel that their views are not taken seriously (Coleman, Catan and Dennison 1997). The issue of power, however, extends much further than the question of 'being taken seriously'.

Indeed, Franklin and Franklin (1990) have identified three dimensions of **ageism** (cultural, political and economic) affecting both young and old people. Central to their argument is the understanding that 'power is not an attribute of individuals but an expression of a relationship between them.' (Franklin and Franklin 1990:5) In addition:

> *Power is not always, although it can be, expressed in dramatic confrontations or battles between powerful individuals, classes, races or nations. It is more commonplace for power relations to become routinised within the life of a society so that overt opposition between dominant and subordinate groups is rare. The most effective exercise of power is a quiet affair in which individuals and groups may be ignorant of their subordination.*
> (Franklin and Franklin 1990:5)

Power relations are also never one dimensional. The ageism experienced by young people may be exacerbated by other forms of oppression deriving from their class, race, gender, sexuality or disability thereby 'creating a complex pattern of relationships of power and subordination.' (Franklin and Franklin 1990:7)

The oppression of young people, therefore, shares a number of common features with other forms of oppression in the sense that it:

- is systematic and structured (e.g. in relation to legal rights)
- is based on stereotypes, prejudices and misconceptions
- operates at personal, cultural, and structural levels (Thompson 1993)
- leads to adverse representation of and discrimination against young people
- acts to exclude young people from aspects of social, political and economic life
- is underpinned by an ideology based on the inherent 'inferiority' of some people (i.e. young and old) because of their age

As Franklin and Franklin observe:

> *Ageism, like racism and sexism, expresses a power relationship between a dominant and subordinate group. The complex package of patronising and prejudicial views about young and old people, which ageism embodies, justifies and sustains many of the injustices which these groups suffer.* (Franklin and Franklin 1990:26)

Yet, despite the social changes (e.g. in the labour market, social security and housing policy) which have affected young people's lives to a point where they are now perceived as 'disadvantaged, whether in the housing market, the labour market or in the overall quest for independence from their parents, (Morrow and Richards 1996:4) young people are still portrayed as a threat to society, not in the political sense of yesteryear, but in terms of the 'social damage they may do through their irresponsible behaviour (e.g. in relation to sex, drugs and delinquency). (Morrow and Richards 1996:4)

Indeed, Wyn and White observe that 'the popular image of young people presenting a 'threat' to law and order presents young people as more powerful than they really are' (Wyn and White 1997:12) – particularly since young people are both 'the symbol of society's future and its victims 'at risk' of succumbing to lives of violence, drug dependence and moral degeneracy.' (Wyn and White 1997:20)

That the term 'youth' has come to signify 'thugs' [car thieves, vandals, hooligans], 'users' [drugs, alcohol, smoking], and 'victims' [unemployment, poor schooling, dysfunctional families], (Jeffs and Smith 1998) none of which are categories, experiences or qualities specific to young people, creates compelling support for the argument that:

> *it is increasingly difficult to approach 'youth' as a meaningful way of categorizing a set of experiences or qualities...[and that since]...'youth' is almost exclusively employed to signify discussion of a social problem or behaviour being portrayed in a negative light...[youth work is]...entwined with a view of young people as being in deficit...[and therefore]...the notion of youth work has a decreasing usefulness.* (Jeffs and Smith 1998:50-61)

All of this being the case, Jeffs and Smith have a point. They also miss the point by virtue of having accepted the contemporary stereotypes of young people as thugs, users and victims. In so doing, they have seen everything that surrounds young people and failed to see young people themselves. That is, young people's own experience of 'being young' in this society. Specifically, their search for identity within the confines of ageism – personal, cultural and structural.

So, whilst it is certainly true that not all 'thugs, users and victims' are young (Jeffs and Smith 1998), it is equally true that young people, nonetheless, share a distinctive experience of being young not least of which is the likelihood that being young increases the chances of being deemed a 'thug, user or victim'. That is the way ageism operates.

If 'youth' is seen as a problem in need of 'surveillance, incarceration and control' (Jeffs and Smith 1998), the question is whether to dispense with it, as we have tried to with the term 'social education' (Smith 1988), or whether to reclaim it within a framework of resistance in much the same way as we have reclaimed 'woman' and 'Black' and more recently the term 'queer' by gay and lesbian activists (e.g. Woods 1995) and 'nigger' by contemporary Black film-makers'. (Pini 1997:162)

This is not to suggest that such terms could possibly hope to convey the richness and complexity of who we are as unique human beings. No single term could. But, in a political sense, such terms act as signifiers offering recognition to our experience and struggle in the face of the personal, cultural and structural oppressions we encounter.

Understanding the experience of 'youth', therefore, lies at the heart of effective youth work. Naming 'youth' provides a focus for young people's experience **as young people** thereby enabling them to confront the contradictions and stereotypes of ageism; and create the possibility for collective action.

'Youth', then, does not need to be dispensed with. It needs to be reclaimed as an active act of resistance.

Identity

Entry into any new period of life involves challenges to an individual's self concept. In other words, a person starts to ask herself or himself questions about the sort of person she or he is. This process involves self reflection in terms of 'social comparison' (how am I like other people; what is my level of worth compared to others?); and exploration of personal values. (Coleman and Hendry 1990)

However, while such self reflection occurs at different significant moments in the course of life, it has been suggested that 'adolescence' represents the first phase of life during which the individual develops a clear personal and social identity that persists throughout life (Coleman and Hendry 1990:82). This being the case, the issue of identity becomes central to a service which targets itself at that precise moment in people's lives.

Also, while accepting the existence of shared patterns of identity development in young people, it needs to be noted that the development of self-concept varies in relation to factors related to social background, whether this is in terms of personal circumstances (e.g. unemployment) or structural factors such as gender or race. (Coleman and Hendry 1990:47). Indeed, it has been argued that not only does 'race' affect identity development but also that young people from Black and white communities actually follow different pathways in becoming aware of their ethnic identity. (Lorenz 1996; Robinson 1997)

However this asymmetry exists for purely social and political reasons, and may be summarised:

> *In the context of a racist society, feeling proud of being Black is not analogous to feeling proud of being white.* (Tizard and Phoenix, quoted in Lorenz 1996:160)

I think it's important for young people to be aware of their identity and to preserve that identity as best they can. My role in that is to enhance their identity and provide information to them. This is what they're asking for and I think as workers it's important that we support it. Not dilute it. This third and fourth generation have now started to call themselves British Muslims. Not Pakistani Muslims or Indian Muslims but British Muslims. That's a political statement that says they were born here. They didn't come from somewhere else. They belong here. They are British and they are Muslim.

But having a clear identity requires an understanding of what it means to be a Muslim. It's a question they have to ask themselves. What it means to them. I'm not there to judge whether they are good or bad Muslims. Nobody can do that. After all, you could have a humanist person who is caring and sharing and a non-Muslim, and still a good person. A good human being. So the same thing goes with the Muslim. You could have someone who is praying five times a day and practising Islam but a good Muslim is what is inside oneself. It's about sharing and caring for other people. And that's really just like being a good human being. So first and foremost the issue is about being a good person.

At the same time, the young people feel themselves to be different. They are concerned about who they are as part of a worldwide Muslim community and what's happening around the world, especially with the Muslims. They are concerned about it and some of them want to be known as Muslims. Others don't because they've seen that it has negative things connected with it. Like a few weeks ago in France there were teachers going on strike because the headmaster allowed a couple of young women to wear head scarves to attend school. The feeling among the young people was 'why are they doing this to us?' And the only reason they come up with is because we are Muslims and we have a different way of life. So the challenge for me as a youth worker is how to turn that into a positive. To look at how we can best contribute within this society that we live in. To contribute to this society as Muslims. Not as non-Muslims. Not as Pakistanis. Yes, young people are interested in visiting Pakistan or Bangladesh and even supporting the Pakistan cricket team. But what they are absolutely clear about is that they are staying here. They are a part of this country. And so they want to contribute to this society as Muslims and be accepted on their terms.

(Abdul Ghaffar)

Within youth work, the development and preservation of identity is, therefore, not about judging young people but rather providing information and supporting them to understand what (for instance) being Muslim means to them. Indeed, in discussing pedagogical principles in the development of anti-racist strategies, Lorenz comments that 'young people have to be facilitated in forming and expressing their ethnic identity, not in adopting given identities'. (Lorenz 1996:161)

> *All my work with young Black people is about enabling them to develop an identity that makes them balanced and operational within this society. When we think of identity we may say that this person is a Black person or dual heritage or whatever concept or notion the European world places upon us as people they see as different. Our choice is to either accept or reject it. For me, one of the most negative aspects of having to embrace the term 'black' in this society is that it doesn't come with any cultural meaning. It's just a political term. It doesn't tell you anything about what it means to be black in this society. So when a young person embraces this concept of being black it becomes a tool that is used to remove them from their true identity. Black is a useful political term. But most other ethnic minority groups move away from that when they are not directly involved in the politics. So if you are from India you are Indian, or from China, Chinese or wherever. You are an indigenous person from that part of the globe. But for people particularly from the Caribbean and Africa that concept of 'blackness' is something which defines us regardless.*

Also, whilst Tajfel observes that ethnic identity is 'that part of an individual's self concept which derives from their knowledge of their membership of a social group (or groups), together with the value and emotional significance attached to that membership' (Tajfel quoted in Lorenz 1996:160), it is easy to see the relevance of such a definition for other 'identities'. In other words, that being gay, or working class, or Jewish (and so on) could equally be described as 'that part of an individual's self concept which derives from their knowledge of their membership of a social group (or groups) together with the value and emotional significance attached to that membership'.

What becomes clear is that supporting young people to form and express their own identity, as opposed to adopting given identities, is a central part of the youth worker's responsibility not only in relation to ethnic identity but also in relation to other identities. In practice, this means providing opportunities for young people to develop both their self-image and self-esteem given that identity or self concept involves a person's:

- self-image – their description of self; or knowledge of membership of a social group
- self-esteem – their evaluation of self; or the value and emotional significance attached to membership of particular social groups (Coleman and Hendry 1990:46).

Self-image (description of self)

We often use residential weekends and festivals to look at contemporary issues. The starting point is usually that week's reading from the Torah – which has been read out at synagogue. What we're asking is what contemporary issues can we draw from this? This becomes quite an astounding experience for the young people because they are confronted with the sense of their religious history and suddenly realise that it may hold some contemporary relevance or dilemmas for them.

Working from an Afrocentric perspective means getting young people to understand that where they are existing now in this time and space is only an eye-blink in the development of humanity. So, therefore, all what is, can change. That's not meant to make them feel insecure about their existence but to help them to understand that the terms you embrace about yourself moves with how you feel about yourself and what power you have. Power is about defining reality and if you have not got the power to define your own reality you are going to be constantly under the control of external factors – racism, sexism, materialism, capitalism, whatever. And, if somebody is layering different aspects of identity on you and you haven't got the tools or knowledge or culture to say 'excuse me, but that isn't me' then you are going to be carrying about all these negative concepts about yourself which you will then internalise and act out.

The background I'm coming from is 18 years in church with my parents frowning upon anything like swearing or talking about sex and then suddenly realising when I was 15 that being gay was a sin you were going to go to hell for according to my parents' religion. Although they know I'm gay they don't really talk about it. So coming to the project is a bit of a relief although I don't think that people here understand what effect 18 years of religion can have on you.

My approach to young men's work is about creating opportunities in a relaxed atmosphere for young men to be more honest and open about themselves and all that comes from that. We have never dangled any carrots in order to get young men involved. We've always made it clear that if they come to the group they'll be expected to talk about themselves and explore what being young men means to them. The interesting thing is that when you create that opportunity to talk the hardest part is getting them to stop talking and listen to each other. It's just like the floodgates have opened because the opportunity is there, perhaps for the first time, to talk about themselves in a reflective rather than superficial way.

Self-esteem (evaluation of self)

Even though youth workers realise that being gay isn't an issue to you, they realise that it can be an issue to other people. Like my parents; they just assume that because I've come out and I'm quite happy and everything that I'm not going to encounter any other problems.

But if I get homophobic abuse and stuff at college – like someone called me lesbian scum the other day in the corridor, the youth workers understand that while it's not affecting me it's something that I take in. And even though they are perfectly chilled out about us all being gay, if one of us comes in really upset because someone has been shouting stuff at us they understand that as well. Whereas my parents just go 'you're all right about being a lesbian aren't you?' and I go 'Yes' and they go 'well what are you worried about then?'

I see everyday in young Black people in their negative behaviour towards each other, how they have internalised the negative aspects of what this society deems as Black. So I very much see my role as helping young people to deconstruct that and look at what their Blackness means to them. What is it that's unique about being in their state of Blackness? What is unique about claiming their Africanity? And when you have tuned into that you can stand up as a more powerful person because you are defining who you actually are based on your knowledge of your history. If young Black people today haven't got that understanding of their history then they are very much confined to a notion of being Black or African as an insignificant thing. That we have never had any power ever as a race of people. That we have done nothing. That we have contributed nothing on the world platform. That we have no history. In fact our history began when the Europeans came and enslaved us. It's all negative. Even the images they get of Africa today is very much about disadvantage, famine, all the negatives in society. So why would you want to associate yourself with that? The term Black becomes a problem because it is an easy option. You can exist in an aspect of Blackness even though it doesn't necessarily support who you actually are.

Once you can deal with that part of your personality which is you being gay, it makes it easier to deal with other stuff – like stuff you may have about your parents of whatever. It's like once I realised I was gay, and even though I was completely chilled out about gay people and everything, I suddenly thought 'Oh my God. I'm gay and I hate myself and I think I'm really ugly and I'm going to have a horrible life and I'm never going to meet anybody.' But once I started coming to the project and being with other gay people and all my friends knew, then everything else didn't seem so bad. It seemed to fall into place.

'Global' self-esteem

In addition, central to young people's changing sense of self is the development of their self-esteem in relation to which 'self theorists' have cast, at the top of the hierarchy of dimensions, a 'global self-esteem' which includes:

- Competence, or success in meeting achievement demands.
- Social acceptance, or attention, worthiness, and positive reinforcement received from significant others.
- Control, or feelings of internal responsibility for outcomes.

- Virtue, or adherence to moral and ethical standards. (Coleman and Hendry 1990:54)

All of which are needs that have for long been addressed and emphasised by youth workers.

Competence, or success in meeting achievement demands

We have an accreditation system in our senior section. Most of this is about moving on. Young women get a certificate in relation to the eight personal development areas identified in the 'Look Wider' programme. Those areas are Out of Doors, International, Independent Living, Sport and Fit for Life, Leadership, Creativity, Service in the Community and Personal Values. When you are in the Guide section, 10–14, you do a selection of these. The words are different but they're the same eight things. When you get to be 14 plus you can specialise or have a particular focus that the unit is trying to work through.

I think it's pretty much accepted that class can adversely affect your success at school. So, part of our role is to compensate by creating opportunities for young people to succeed. That's not saying that working class young people have more, or more important needs than middle class young people. I think it's just that the needs of the two groups are different. I have to admit, though, that middle class young people are more likely than working class young people to be able to sort out their own issues or problems. Or certainly that they tend to have more people and resources around them to help them sort out those things.

Social acceptance, or attention, worthiness, and positive reinforcement received from significant others

When we're talking about the development of social skills, what we're often talking about is the kind of social skills that working class young people need to help them deal with people of a middle class background. Frequently, it's about gaining the confidence to engage with or deal with people in authority or people they think are more important than they are. So you are often in situations with them where you have to be saying 'You're just as important as everybody else in this queue or everybody else trying to see this person. Don't put yourself down'. As a youth worker, you have to find different ways of saying this but basically it's about getting young people to value themselves and have the confidence to believe they are as important as anybody else. When we are not directly addressing it we are doing so indirectly by encouraging young people to do things that increase their confidence and make them look important to others.

Taking a group of young people to Egypt helped that group of young people to shift their sense of self and their understanding of their people's contribution to the world stage. There was a level of pride and dignity that was nurtured within the group as they began to explore their connection with Egypt and their understanding of Egypt as an ancient and prominent civilisation. Young Black people need to be given experiences and encounters with Africa which can enhance their self-concept and develop a positive sense of self.

Control, or feelings of internal responsibility for outcomes

I started off as a trouble-maker when I was a junior. Now I'm a volunteer leader at the junior club and I can see what I used to do. I can see the thing from both sides now. I'm lucky being on the leadership training programme because it makes me explore who I am although it's kind of scary because it has come around so quickly. But I've definitely changed as a person. I can criticise myself now as a leader and it helps me with communication and gives me a good experience because I love being with the little kids.

We are there to offer clarity and help young people understand the consequences of their actions. We provide a safe environment for them to deal with the conflicts of self that they may have.

Virtue, or adherence to moral and ethical standards

The operating world view as it relates to practice is paramount within my approach to youth work. Young people of African heritage need to experience positive encounters with African culture as part of the journey which aids the positive development of their identity. There need to be opportunities for young Black people to critically analyse their belief systems, enabling them to explore how their current beliefs are affecting their perception, cognition and knowledge. Contrasting the consequences of differing belief systems introduces alternatives for young people that lead to development and growth, leaving young people in the position of making conscious choices and accepting responsibility for them.

That volunteering has survived for young people is nothing short of a miracle, given Thatcher's Britain in which the question that was always asked is 'what's in it for me?' But I think the reason they've pulled through is partly because of their Jewish values and sense of community and continuity.

The body 'inscribed'

However, the 'fashioning of identity' is not simply a matter of being a man or woman; Black or white since, as Foucault (1988) observes, it is not the 'physical body' which has meaning but the particular cultural and historical contexts within which the meaningless body becomes 'raced' or 'gendered'. It is the cultural and historical *context* rather than the body itself which gives rise to meaning and therefore identity. A context within which 'bodies' have already been 'coded' as a result of being classified and regulated by ourselves and others. For example, in the way that the female body has been coded as 'hysterical', the Black body as 'deviant' the teenage body as 'rebellious', the disabled body as 'invalid' (Pini 1997:158). For this reason:

> *The process of young people's growing self-identity and definition involves knowing not only 'who they are' but also 'who they are not'. That means sifting the messages that permeate the social system to understand what they are 'told' about who they are and making sense of this in the context of their own experiences, thoughts and feelings.*

Or, as expressed by Erich Fromm: 'Unless I am able to analyse the unconscious aspects of the society in which I live, I cannot know who I am, because I do not know which part of me is **not** me.' (1993:78)

The process of their developing identity, therefore, forces young people to confront the ways in which 'their body' (and the bodies of others) has been classified, 'inscribed' and regulated within the context of ageism, racism, sexism, and the other structural inequalities and institutionalised oppressions which exist. That is, the ways in which people are perceived and treated because they are, for example, women in a sexist society, Black people in a racist society or young people in an ageist society, since it is from within this context that young people engage in the process of 'making sense' of themselves, their lives and their world.

Young people are influenced by their peers. But I think they are also searching for an identity or individuality that says I'm part of this group but I'm still that little bit different. We often talk about peer groups but we don't often talk about young people as individuals within that. And actually in any group you'll find a dynamic range of people who have a lot in common but also have a lot of things that are different about them.

To me, racism represents ten to fifteen years of painful transition. Years of explaining to your elders and arguing with your colleagues. I'm not sure it represents that for most young Black people today. So I understand the impact of what racism does to people not only from my own experience but also from the way young people understand it. And actually, because they did not experience that painful historical transition, they are much more confident about their ability to cope and deal with it. They have a sense of being able to play the system, work it, beat it, sidestep it. And, while I may not necessarily agree with young people's agenda on how to deal with these political issues, I have to accept that this is how they see it and how they experience it. Their attitude is very much 'this is how it is now, deal with it'. That makes them very much more pragmatic than I ever was.

cont...

The importance of who you are, where you've come from and your roots is strongly grounded in our sense of community and continuity. Young people have that now. It's not necessarily something they had to discover. It's a way of life that goes without saying. A legacy that they've been given of right. So, when you ask them to think about home and what goes on there and who their role models are, they can tell you. That provides them with a platform from which to move on. When I listen to young adults or young people talk about it and the history of the people who they think made them, it really is awesome because they can stand proud without the tears and the pain. They can express their point without the emotion I had to keep bottled up. They can see a vision based on the black pearls of wisdom they were given as children and the history of our people which has informed them and given them self belief in what they can do.

(Joy Scott Thompson)

'Morally textured landscape'

While work around specific identities is central to youth work practice there is also another, equally important, aspect of identity. That is the recognition that identity or self-concept concerns not only the question of what it means to be, for example, Jewish or Christian, or male, or Black or gay, but also the question of what it means to be 'a person'. Therefore, when we understand identity as involving a person's self-image and self-esteem, we are referring not only to their membership of social group(s) but also, and importantly, to their description and evaluation of self as 'a person' – as a human being.

In addition, since humans are by nature social beings, our identities are inevitably a function of our social relations. Therefore, in order to sustain our identities we must 'morally respect' both the identities, of those around us and the social relations which sustain those identities. (Shotter 1993:164) Indeed, according to Shotter, in order to qualify as citizens we must perceive ourselves as being in a 'morally textured landscape'. We must understand how we are currently 'placed or positioned' in that landscape and operate from an awareness that 'opportunities for action' are made differentially available because of our location. (1993:162)

Identity is, therefore, a question of morals. Not simply because virtue (adherence to moral and ethical standards) is a crucial dimension of self-esteem, but because we are social beings living in a 'morally textured landscape'. A landscape that requires us to understand our moral responsibility to ourselves and others. A landscape that requires us to develop, through our changing sense of self, a consistent set of values and the virtue that makes us authentic human beings.

On values and virtue

Morality, however, cannot be understood as a set of universally valid rules since moral action requires choices to be made – not simply in choosing whether to steal or not to steal; to lie or not to lie – but in the more complex weighing of one 'good' (e.g. loyalty) against another 'good' (e.g. justice). In the process of such deliberations, we come to recognise the necessity for rational judgement within a 'coherent system of precepts'. (Williamson 1997:97)

Youth work is not, therefore, concerned with the inculcation of a prescribed set of values but rather with the development of young people's critical skills and rational judgement; and their disposition towards a 'coherent system of precepts' which underpin the exercise of such judgements.

In other words, youth work's intention is to enable and support young people to develop the critical skills and moral dispositions needed to make rational judgements and choices that they can sustain through committed action.

This is not, however, a solitary activity since:

> The moral self is nurtured in social contexts and develops through learning and through being a member of, and living within, a society and making the moral decisions which are inescapably part of being a sentient human being. (Williamson 1997:103)

Indeed, it is primarily through such shared 'moral inquiry' that people are enabled to develop an understanding of their moral nature as human beings. Youth work can, therefore, be understood as the engagement of young people in the 'moral inquiry' or deliberations integral to their development as moral human beings – where morality is seen as being concerned with:

- conduct in relation to people's well-being
- some degree of freedom of choice
- impartiality – which should apply equally to all persons in similar circumstances (Barrow 1981)

This is not, however, an easy task, particularly given the constant tension between the needs of the individual and the needs of the 'state' – conceptualised by Aristotle in terms of whether education should:

- develop the potential for excellence in each individual or their ability to serve the good of the polis (an ancient Greek city-state)

- promote the noblest life or the most comprehensive civic life
- promote the education of the free citizen who is capable of deliberating while giving directions to those unsuited for self-rule (Rorty 1993:35)

Notwithstanding, social education within youth work has always attempted to balance 'individual self-expression with a degree of conformity'. (Davies and Gibson 1967:17) A tension which exists to the present day.

> *What I want is for young people to grow up to be responsible members of society and that they share and care. The reason that they should share and care is because it works. It's basically the Christian message. Love your neighbour as yourself. Society will work but you need to give a bit. It's actually the very opposite of the Enterprise Culture with which we are now all imbued and which says 'what are you volunteering for, aren't you good enough to get paid?'*

> *A residential is the best place to think about how you treat other people – which is basically where all values start because it's no good having wonderful global values about equal opportunities if you can't get on with the people around you. It is also an important place for young people to learn to be in control. It's a chance for them to come out of their norms into a different set of norms. Very often it's a chance for them to feed themselves. And that's quite a big thing for young women today because most of them don't actually do a lot of cooking at home. Then there's the activities and all the social time which is when the conversations really happen – around preparing the meal, eating it and all the other things that have to be done.*

> *We were playing softball with a group of kids in the park and this guy did this freaky shot and it went way out of the park and through someone's car window. It was quite interesting because there was nobody around and the young people were going 'Right, quick let's run'. And the part-time youth worker who was there said 'No I don't think we can do that. We broke this car window and we have to take responsibility.' And that created a really good debate, at the end of which they left a note. Those kinds of situations is really what it's about. Enabling young people to know what's right and wrong. And, hopefully, helping them to make choices that are going to be positive to other people*

However, while some would argue that not all values are moral values, all values are, nonetheless, based fundamentally on some conception of what is 'right' or what is 'good'. Or, as Milton Rokeach put it, 'an enduring belief that a specific mode of conduct or end state of existence is personally or socially preferable to an opposite or converse mode of conduct or end state of existence' (1973:5). In other words, that telling the truth, for example, is preferable to lying or deliberately misleading others as a 'mode of conduct'. And that justice, for example, is preferable to injustice as 'an end state of existence'.

The challenge for youth work is how to develop a practice which:

- addresses values without 'imposing' them

- maintains a meaningful and appropriate concern for individual as well as societal needs
- enables young people to engage in 'moral inquiry'
- supports young people's disposition towards virtue
  - as a central dimension of their self-esteem
  - as social beings in a morally textured landscape

Values without 'imposition'

Engaging with young people in their social education is a privilege and a luxury. So you have to be very careful that you don't impose your own standards and values on them. That's where it becomes really skilful because you can't deny your own beliefs and values. But if you acknowledge them and are aware of where you are coming from then you stand a better chance of working effectively from your value base without imposing your view on young people.

For a long time now the youth service has been conscious of not wanting to just pass on a prescribed set of values. Yet, at the same time, we talk about youth workers being role models. The thing is young people don't choose as role models people who have no values or principles. They choose people they can identify with and that's often based on some moral or spiritual quality they respect. In fact one of the most common things that African-Caribbean, African, Asian young people have is some sort of faith or spiritual involvement that comes from their home and culture. It doesn't matter what religion the young people are. It's about faith and a belief in something that underpins the way they live their life and makes them as a person.

The individual and society

Most of the time people think that the universe is miles out there. But the truth is that you can go in and in and in as much as you can go out and out and out. Everything in the universe is connected. All the things we think of as being out there and all the things we think of as being in here. They are all connected. Some scientist said that in your lifetime every individual on earth is likely to breathe a cell of Jesus. And if you think about it, when you sneeze millions of cells of your body are propelled into the universe and some cells are immutable, they just go up into the air and are carried on the stratosphere and drop down somewhere else. And they become part of everything else. So, if you drop a piece of litter, you

cont...

make that area unpleasant. But, if you didn't drop it and your friend sees you put the litter in your pocket instead, you will have set an example and your friend might do the same. And in that moment you will have changed the universe. So I think what we are really about is changing the universe.

I was originally trained in religious life as a Franciscan friar, and my basic philosophy when I came into youth work was the principle of the Franciscans – that basically all you need to do to get to Heaven is to keep the Commandments and love your neighbour: don't pinch his things and take responsibility. If you want to do something else, Jesus said 'Go and give all you have to the poor and come and follow me.' The Franciscans take that to mean 'do what I do'. So, as a youth worker, my message to young people is that we don't need to know anything else to be happy. Love your neighbour, take responsibility and basically give. And the more you give, the more you'll get.

Christian values are not the values just of Christians. They are the values that Christ put over to us. People sometimes mix that up because what has happened is that different individuals and groups have taken what Jesus said and changed and adapted it to suit their own interests – particularly in terms of power. What Jesus said was 'This is the way we should behave as individuals to make a better society'. That is not the same as the values of the Church that has tortured people, had wars and done a whole load of other things.

(Kevin Murphy)

Moral inquiry

One of the most basic Jewish values is to question your surroundings. A good illustration of this is a part of Jewish religious law called the 'Mishna'. This is where you have a piece of text from the Torah in the middle of the page surrounded by eight to ten commentaries from different sources. Some of them agreeing with each other. Some completely disagreeing. There is page after page of this and the premise is that all these commentaries are right. In fact, in orthodox Jewish seminaries they sit from eight in the morning to eight at night, day after day, arguing over the same piece of text. Debate is seen as a very good thing.

Most young people do not know what they believe, morality and ethics is not a curriculum subject in GCSEs. They behave in a way that is part of a group but when you ask them what do you actually believe they find it hard to express. For example, a young woman may not know that she values life and therefore disagrees with abortion until she is actually pregnant and faced with the dilemma of 'do I have an abortion or carry on with the pregnancy?' If this is the point at which she discovers that she does not agree with abortion then it could be said that she has no choice in the matter. Whereas, if she knew beforehand that she values life, she may have taken greater responsibility of her reproductive creative powers and viewed that aspect of her creativity as sacred and therefore taken precautions so as not to get pregnant. So, what youth work can do is help young people put their beliefs and values to the test in a safe way.

Disposition towards virtue

Whilst it has always been the case that some commitments to virtue arise from specifically religious values, Barrow maintains that we should engage in moral behaviour for its own sake, not out of fear or self-interest, or because we have been told to do so. '*Good* exists independently of God and, therefore, morality does not depend on religion for its existence.' (1981:144)

> *I believe that a good person does good for themselves and others. It's not just a one-sided thing. That means having a positive attitude about your own life and towards other people. It means making a positive contribution to your community or neighbourhood and, if you have the energy, contributing in a wider way. Good people share their good practice with others and show others how they have become good.*

Virtues and virtue

Virtues refer to **particular** moral qualities, for example, wisdom, courage, benevolence, compassion or trustworthiness.

By contrast, virtue is 'an ethically admirable **disposition** of character…[which] helps to determine, in the right contexts, what one will want to do.' (Williams, 1993:9) Virtue, therefore, requires that a person will choose to act in certain ways based on a disposition towards certain ideals. Virtue asks not 'what should I do?' but 'what would the just or compassionate or trustworthy or courageous or 'virtuous' person do?'

The practice of virtue, therefore, requires the ability to make judgements and take action whilst being guided by some underlying set of values or ethical principles – whether they have their origins, as suggested by the workers here, in specifically religious beliefs, are considered to be part of an innate moral reality, or are the result of reason.

> *We are trying to merge two different sets of values. A set of values that is Jewish in orientation which have a lot of history and heritage – which relate to people's everyday lives and is relevant to young people in the modern world. We merge this with a youth work ethos, which is similar and has the same value base, but in some ways conflicts. For example, a youth worker's value*

base for discussing alcohol might be one of providing information, pointing out the dangers to people and so on. The Jewish angle on alcohol is in some ways similar to that since the basis of us living here is we should be healthy people. But actually alcohol is an integral part of Jewish ritual. So you can't just say to young Jewish people that alcohol is a no-go because on a Friday night where there is some level of Jewish observance, wine is a part of the ritual so we have to try to find a way of merging those two ways of thinking.

There are two kinds of morality. We have laws in society which set a kind of morality and we have conscience. I believe that conscience is innate. That is, you come into the world knowing all and you lose it through the processes we go through. But that inner morality is not a set of rules to follow. It is a recognition of the sacredness of life and our relationship to everything as complementary.

As a child you often accept your parents' view of the world. And that view is really the conclusion that they have come to about life. Then, as you get older, you start to test out, with other people, the views you've acquired from home to see whether they are right or real. To see what other alternatives there may be around. What the youth worker does is to provide opportunities for young people to engage in that questioning and testing out. So the worker may be used as a kind of sounding board. Or the worker may be a source of alternative views. Not necessarily their own views but maybe a range of alternatives. I remember having discussions with young people about Black people coming over here and taking jobs. They would have no thought about why and how that may have happened, the inconsistencies with what their parents were saying, the contradictory stereotypes that, on the one hand said Black people are lazy and good for nothing, and on the other hand they were taking all the jobs and were hard working and so on. These young people had no experience of somebody actually encouraging them to explore what all that meant. So, as you become an adult, you examine the views and values that you have been given by your parents. That doesn't mean that you necessarily reject them because sometimes you realise that maybe once or twice your parents were saying the right thing or there were things that you would want to keep. But you've actually made a decision about them as opposed to just accepting them. The role of the youth worker in all of that is to help young people to reflect on their life experiences and think about how their learning from one situation transfers to another situation. So, if they're saying to me that they want to be a positive person who contributes to society, then what they have to understand is how their actual behaviour in different situations fits in with this helpful, kind, sharing person that they say they want to be. The issue becomes one of consistency. Trying to develop a consistent sense of self in terms of their core attitudes, values and beliefs. Then, when they make decisions about what is right or wrong, and these may be tough decisions, they are able to make them because they have a consistent set of values that enable them not only to make the decision but also to implement it. So their values provide a guide in terms of the things they would do as well as the things they couldn't possibly see themselves doing.

Such perspectives are common not only in youth work but in life generally since different people have different ideas about what is 'right' and 'wrong', and, importantly, different beliefs about how we come to 'know' what is right and wrong; and how we ought to behave as a result. But these ideas do not come to us from nowhere. In fact, moral philosophy (ethics – the study of moral values and human moral conduct) represents one of the main branches of philosophy which dates back at least five thousand years to the time of ancient Mesopotamia.

Obviously, this book cannot even begin to chart that journey of developing thought. The main point here is to recognise that contemporary beliefs about the moral content of human conduct and the principles that should govern it are part of long and rich ethical traditions about which much has already been, and will continue to be, written. For our purpose here, we must be content with simply illuminating the traditions identified by workers in the quotations above. That is religious ethical traditions, innate or natural moral order and rational judgement. In so doing, two things become clear.

Firstly, that despite their different perspectives about the origins or source of morality, the qualities considered to be virtues tend to be widely shared among different ethical traditions. Particularly, virtues such as kindness, compassion, benevolence, forgiveness, wisdom, courage, trustworthiness, justice, humility and honourable dealings between people.

Secondly, whether 'greater wisdom' is thought to come from one's God or some natural moral order in the universe, virtue is nonetheless achieved through human endeavour. That is to say, virtue is not a set of rules to be followed unthinkingly. Virtue requires practical reason. Human beings must deliberate about what we think we **ought** to do; and make judgements about what we will actually do. The development of virtue, therefore, involves a process of reflection through which we perfect our own moral character. Indeed, it was Socrates' opinion that 'the unexamined life' was not worth living – that to be good 'the good life' must have reflection as a part of its goodness. (cited in Williams, 1993:21)

Religious traditions

For the most part, I think young people absorb values without making sense of them. Without thinking about them. Life kind of happens to them in a rather random way. That's why, when they come up against something that's different, like the work we do here, it's so important because they are then forced to question the path that's been laid out for them. They start to look at themselves and their lives and kind of think 'Is this what

cont...

I want?' That question is not as common as it could be. It takes a lot of work to get a young person to think that around here. In fact, I think most young people I've met here in the last eight years either just want to make sure that they have a job, any job, or have the most unbelievably high and unrealistic aspirations. There is very little in between.

Something that's specific to young Jewish people, and perhaps other religious groups, is the sense of a life cycle. There is an annual Jewish cycle, a monthly, a weekly cycle, a daily cycle for some and it's very specific. A lot of young Jewish people have this as a value but they are not conscious of it because they have never known anything else. So, for example, they will know that every September is the New Year, whether they observe it or not. They know Friday and Saturday is Shabbat. Whether they choose to go out on a Friday night or choose to observe Shabbat they know it exists and they know it is significant because they are Jewish. There is Bar Mitzvah, which is a very significant event whether they choose to observe it or not – and most of them do. All of this provides 'markers' that affect their values because life is not just one long thing. In that sense, they are used to being 'boundaried'. That is having some level of prescriptive boundary. And, whether they choose to observe it or not, they know that boundary is there and fundamentally affects their lives.

Lots of the young people don't have a specifically Jewish identity. They come to the centre because their friends come and their friends are Jewish. It's not a conscious thing even though they have made a choice to be cultural specific by attending this particular centre. In fact, sometimes when we are interviewing volunteers, we ask them why, as a Jew, they have chosen to work with young Jewish people. And it's an extraordinary question for them. Their heads blow off and they go 'Oh have I? Did I choose that?'

Some people would say that there are no specifically Jewish values – just human values. But I think the Jewish take includes continuity. So the average, intelligent, questioning aware human being who wants to question themself and their actions and the actions of other people – if that person is Jewish – also has another layer of religious understanding of themself as part of a continuum which recognises those who went before and those who will come after. This is absolutely lodged in the Jewish unconscious. At 16 or 17, young people are becoming aware of this and their role in the Jewish community as part of the Jewish chain. So we get a lot of young

cont...
people, and adults, who want to be volunteer workers because, in their words, they want to put something back into the community. And even though they may not identify it in a conscious way, it is still a recognition of the Jewish life cycle and the significance of continuity.

(Myra Topper)

Within Judaism the pursuit of virtue rests on the imitation of God since God is good and, therefore, to be good is to be like Him.

> *Since human beings are created in the image of God, it is obvious that one achieves the highest possible level of perfection or self-realisation by becoming as similar to God as humanly possible. This is the basis of what may be the single most important ethical doctrine of the Hebrew Bible, that of 'imitatia Dei', the imitation of God...One achieves holiness (that is) by obeying God's commandments or...by walking in his ways.* (Kellner, 1993:84)

For the Christians it is a case of obeying God's commandments whilst 'walking in the ways' of Jesus Christ – of showing forgiveness, loving kindness, mercy, compassion, charity, justice, faith, and, most importantly, humility. However, the Golden Rule – 'do unto others as you would have them do unto you' – is not simply a command to follow some specific rule, but rather a requirement to think and deliberate about what each situation demands. (Preston 1993)

So, whilst religions have established rules or principles of ethical behaviour, for example, the Judeo-Christian Ten Commandments, the Buddhist Noble Eightfold Path, the Five Pillars of Islam, it is also clear that the development of virtue is considered to rest not only on devotion to some greater wisdom, but also on the exercise of human reason.

> *While revealing his will to humankind in the Quran, God also urges them to exercise reason in understanding revelation...Like Judaism and Christianity, Islam's beginnings are [thus] rooted in the idea of the divine command as a basis for establishing moral order through human endeavour.* (Nanji 1993:107)

Indeed, whilst the Noble Eightfold Path contains within it a wide range of sanctions and prohibitions covering all aspects of human life and conduct (Saddhatissa 1987; Khema, 1987), it is, in essence, a threefold scheme of moral training which consists of:

- the development of wisdom – right understanding, right thought
- the practice of virtues – right speech, right conduct, right livelihood

- the practice of meditation – right effort, right mindfulness, right contemplation

Thus, in Buddhist ethics, there is a close integration of the ethical as a rational engagement of analysis and argument, as a normative recommendation of conduct and a way of life, as a social expression and as an intense personal quest and mode of character development.
(De Silva 1993:59)

Natural moral order

Confucius[1], believing in a natural moral order, subscribed to the ancient Chinese conception of Tao – The Way – the sum total of truths about the universe and humanity in the form of the individual and society. For Confucius, virtue (te) was scripted in Heaven to be cultivated by human beings. Confucian virtues include benevolence, wisdom, courage (when guided by morality), trustworthiness and righteousness, although Confucius believed that 'the only worthwhile thing a man can do is to become as good a man as possible' for its own sake. (1979:12)

Similarly, Mencius[2] postulated that all people are born with four incipient tendencies in 'germ' or seed form – compassion, which is the germ of benevolence; a sense of shame, the germ of dutifulness; courtesy and modesty, the germ of observance of the rites, and right and wrong, the germ of wisdom. (Mencius 1970:82) For Mencius, these four 'germs' constitute the 'original heart' which must be cared for, nurtured and cultivated in order to grow to full maturity. The purpose of the heart is to think and it is this, according to Mencius, which distinguishes human beings from animals. Therefore, through our own effort, human beings can perfect our own moral characters.

Also, like his teacher Plato[3], who believed in an unchanging unwritten 'law' to which all human behaviour is subject, Aristotle[4] was also committed to natural justice 'which has the same authority everywhere, and is independent of opinion.'

---

1. Confucius (K'ung Chung-ni) was a Chinese philosopher who lived from 551–479 BC The Analects are a collection of his sayings compiled by his students shortly after his death.
2. Mencius (Meng K'e) was a Chinese philosopher who was probably born a century or so after the death of Confucius and likely to have died by the end of the fourth century BC. The Mencius was written in the years just after 320 BC
3. Plato was a Greek philosopher, and student of Socrates, who lived from about 428–348 BC.
4. Aristotle was a Greek philosopher and student of Plato who lived from 384–322 BC.

(Aristotle, 1987:167). He also believed that virtue lies in the degree to which 'reason' is or is not the ruling faculty in a person's being.

It is perfectly clear that it is the rational part of man (sic) which is the man himself, and that it is the virtuous man who feels the most affection for this part. (Aristotle 1987:309)

However, while producing an extensive catalogue of virtues (including courage, temperance, wisdom and justice), Aristotle considered justice to be the supreme virtue.

Justice...is not a part of virtue but the whole of virtue; its opposite, injustice not a part of vice but the whole of vice. (Aristotle 1987:146)

Therefore, the virtue of justice was considered to underpin all other virtues as well as provide the basis for deliberation and 'right reason'. And, while Gilligan's (1982) theory of an ethic of care maintained that men (more so than women) conceive of morality as being based on justice whereas women (more so than men) conceive of morality as being based on caring for others, the plain fact is that every moral decision contains not only principle but also a context which, by its very nature, includes specific circumstances and relationships. Therefore, taken together an ethic of justice and an ethic of care create a conception of morality within which:

the moral person is seen as one whose moral choices reflect reasoned and deliberate judgements that ensure justice be accorded each person while maintaining a passionate concern for the well-being and care of each individual. (Brabeck 1993:48)

So, whilst some conceptualise virtue from a specifically religious base and others subscribe to an innate or natural moral order in the universe, both perspectives affirm the need for human beings to think and deliberate about what each situation demands and exercise human reason. In other words, that the development of virtue requires the exercise of practical reason and rational judgement by autonomous human beings – that is people capable of acting in accordance with reason and from their own free will, voluntarily as opposed to acting 'under compulsion or from ignorance.' (Aristotle 1987:66)

Practical reason

The primary advocate of 'pure reason', Immanuel Kant[5], postulated that a good will is the only unconditioned good, and the purpose of reason is to produce a will that is good in itself as opposed to a will that is good as a means to something else.

---

5. Immanuel Kant, German philosopher 1724–1804.

Kant's categorical imperative was that people should 'act only on that maxim through which you can at the same time will that it should become a universal law' (i.e. **will** that everyone should behave in the same way). In other words, if I believe that it is OK for me to steal, then (as a universal law) I must also be prepared to accept (or will) that it is OK for you to steal…and OK for you to steal from me. Kant's categorical imperative is, therefore, not a prescription for behaviour but a principle to be used in making rational moral judgements.

Also, since a rational person is one who acts in accordance with principles, then, according to Kant, one reasons one's way to morality through the exercise of practical reason, or, in other words, through one's will. (Kant, 1948).

Benn and Peters (1959) suggest that Kant's categorical imperative is actually underpinned by three principles:

1. Impartiality – that is, impartial consideration of people as sources of needs, claims and interests.

2. Respect for people as rational human beings – as illustrated in Kant's subordinate maxim 'treat humanity, whether in your own person or in the personal of any other, never simply as a means, but always at the same time as an end' (Kant 1948).

3. Autonomy – 'act as if you were, through your maxims, a law-making member of a kingdom of ends' (Kant 1948) which, according to Benn and Peters, demonstrates Kant's commitment to individual autonomy that also takes account of others' like moral status.

Notwithstanding, utilitarian philosophers dispute the idea that morality could be based on pure reason. For them, a thing can only be good if it is good for someone. Actions are, therefore, perceived as right or wrong according to the extent to which they promote the greatest good for the greatest number – usually construed as the greatest pleasure or happiness. (Bentham 1948)[6] In other words, according to their consequences as opposed to their motive. However, in deciding between our own happiness and that of others, it is necessary to be impartial and so utilitarianism requires the basic principle of benevolence. (Benn and Peters, 1959)

Even by the utilitarian code, then, one is still required to make some judgement about what would constitute the greatest good however conceptualised. Therefore, utilitarianism requires not only benevolence but also some level of practical reason and rational judgement by autonomous human beings regardless of whether the motive is to exercise virtue for its own sake, or to bring about some particular consequence – i.e. the greatest good for the greatest number.

---

6. Jeremy Bentham, English philosopher 1748–1832.

However, the question is:

> *not simply how am I to conduct myself in my life, but how am I to become the kind of person readily disposed so to conduct myself, the kind of person for whom proper conduct emanates characteristically from a fixed disposition?* (Kosman 1980:103)

Learning to be virtuous

According to social psychologists Piaget (1932) and Kohlberg, (1981; 1983) the process of moral development comes in a sequence of overlapping stages, both cognitive and emotional, during which young people learn to structure the way they think about rules and moral issues. The process, for Piaget, is basically a transformation away from a situation where rules are given by an external authority and, for Kohlberg, obeyed through fear of punishment; to a situation where rules are consciously deliberated and negotiated by the individual, [Piaget] who also seeks to establish universal principles through their own experience and critical thought [Kohlberg]. (Pring 1984)

The process, therefore, moves beyond simple habituation to a concern, not only with the existence of certain rules, but, more centrally, with the general principles on which these rules are based.

> *In every family there are those pearls of wisdom. The maxims you were constantly being told by your parents. As adults we often think that young people ignore them. But I don't think that's true. I think young people hold on to the same pearls of wisdom that their parents gave them. Even if they're just lodged in their minds. And those principles form the key elements that make up their life. What they are searching for is a way to move on from there. Perhaps discarding some of those pearls and establishing new ones or new interpretations that match their lives and the person they want to be as a part of this society. What they want is to please their parents, carers, the people to whom they are accountable, while also feeling valued and valuable. But what makes them valued to a parent isn't necessarily what makes them valued to a peer. So they struggle. A youth worker has to take all of this on board.*

> *Young people are aware of the confusions and contradictions of life. What they are trying to do is put together a jigsaw puzzle without the picture on the box. They may even have a lot of the pieces but they still feel that they are not doing it properly. They are searching for some answers. For instance, their family may go to church and they themselves may be holding on to some of those beliefs. Yet, at the same time, they may be doing all sorts of things that are against what their family thinks. When you talk to them they might say that they believe in the bible. They'll tell you 'OK I never read it and I don't go to church but it doesn't mean I disregard it. Just because I don't use it in the way you want me to use it, youth worker, or mother or church leader, doesn't mean that I don't regard it.' The issue is*

not about judging young people or their actions. It's about listening to them and understanding how they are using the knowledge, ethical principles, beliefs and values they have acquired to inform their own lives.

However, in order to utilise 'knowledge, ethical principles, beliefs and values' to inform one's life one must necessarily be capable of making reasoned judgements. This is the basis of autonomy, not only in the sense of freedom of will or regard for the like moral status of others, but also in terms of:

- An attitude to authority and 'taken for granted' rules that, though respectful of them, becomes increasingly questioning of the principles behind the rules.
- An increasing integration of the values and purposes that permeate one's actions and relationships.
- A sense of one's own value and identity through different circumstances and pressures. (Pring, 1984:75)

And, following John Dewey, while people may inherit certain moral principles from their family and community, they can nonetheless 'through rational inquiry, devise new solutions to social problems, working consciously together to reform their community and their own moral outlooks.' (Schneewind 1993:154)

Being second or third generation African-Caribbean or African in this country means that the connection, traditions and values that perhaps their parents or grandparents had are now being recreated and coming up in a new format for the young people today. That can be both a good and a bad thing because, obviously, culture is always evolving, therefore it's a moving thing and not a stagnant thing. So when I see young people re-asserting a black culture and identity in a way that's different from how young people asserted it when I was young, I think that's a good thing. But what can be lost in that is the core values from which your culture is derived. And I think sometimes it's the core values that help maintain you as a person when there's chaos and mayhem going on around you. If your values are sure then that supports any kind of choices in life that you seek to make.

I know the damage that has been done to Black people in thinking that we have to change or assimilate our values because European values and white middle-class values are somehow better than ours. So concepts of parenting and all the other values that we came with have somehow been dissipated into a place where there are no boundaries for young people. Some people see that as liberating but I truly feel that for you to feel secure in this society you have to be held – not in a cage – but something that is holding you and supporting you. I don't see being ultra liberal as support. I see it as being negligent in fact. Because, in order for us to feel whole and operate effectively, we need to go through a process of understanding not only our rights but also our responsibilities and our connection to humanity.

Right action and right motive

There are, therefore, two basic issues of virtue:
- how to find right action in particular circumstances
- how to act from right motive (Preston 1993:93)

Finding right action

Central to 'finding right action' is the ability to make reasoned choices and yet:

> *No doubt for many of us, much of the time, the reasons that lie behind our actions are muddled, insufficiently worked out or only vaguely formulated in our minds. Nonetheless, we choose to act in some ways rather than others and our choices are based on reason – for to make a choice is precisely to opt for one thing rather than another for some kind of reason.* (Barrow 1975:21)

'Finding right action', therefore, requires the individual, firstly, to accept that she or he has choices, however limited or constrained they may be; and secondly, be able to *make* choices based on reasoned and rational judgement. This is a continuous lifelong process since virtue is not:

> *an eternal quality of an unchanging good human being, but a disposition of character that is able to select and practice the good within the recognition that authenticity of action is related to multiple dimensions of selfhood and self-transcending behaviour.* (Streng 1993:98)

'Finding right action' is also a process nurtured in social contexts (Williamson 1997) and therefore, in order to discover and develop authentic virtuous expression, two conditions are needed:

1. A process of dialogue between sincere people who represent different ideologies – with each participant in the dialogue attempting 'to evoke the best, the deepest, the most enlightening aspects of the dialogue partner's orientation… instead of looking for ways to discredit it'.
2. The learning and cultivation of virtuous expression by practice as well as by testing and exploring in dialogue. (Streng 1993:99-100)

Indeed, it was Aristotle who commented that 'it is not enough to know the nature of virtue; we must endeavour to possess it, and to exercise it, and to use whatever other means are necessary for becoming good.' (Aristotle 1987:351)

In this sense, 'dialogue' is envisaged not so much as a Socratic question and answer interrogation designed to uncover 'universal truths' but more as a 'conversation' in which young people are supported to know what **they** think, by being able to 'see' what they say. (Weick 1995) A conversation involving mutual respect and freedom of rationality. A 'conversation' particularly important to young people given that 'adolescence' represents the first phase of life during which they begin to develop a clear personal and social identity. (Coleman and Hendry 1990) However, as Midgley observes:

> *Discussing – serious, open-minded discussing rather than just disputing – is not easy. It is something that people need to learn to do while they are still young and flexible…that discussion is inevitably philosophical. Philosophy, in fact, is not a luxury. At least in confusing times like ours, philosophy is an unavoidable necessity.* (Midgley 1997:38)

Acting from right motive

Acting from right motive is not merely a question of dialogue and reflection. Acting from right motive requires attention to feelings as well as thought for, as David Hume argued, morality 'must be rooted in our feelings since morality moves us to action, and reason alone can never do so'. (Cited in Schneewind 1993:150) As one worker remarks:

> *Maliciousness, downright cruelty, racism – and OK this sounds all pat – racism, sexism and so on, but I am quite serious. If someone makes a racist remark when we are in the minibus then there's no real discussion. That's out of line. It's unacceptable. You will not do that. You will not shout racist remarks out of the minibus. And then, after you've done that bit, then it's time for talking. There are times when values are very straight forward.*

Youth work

Why is a discussion about moral philosophy, values and virtue, important to youth work?

Because 'moral inquiry' through conversation and the cultivation of virtuous expression through practise are the processes through which youth workers enable young people to gain the critical abilities necessary to make rational judgements which affirm the values and virtues they accept, after deliberation, as constituting the kind of people they want to be, the kind of relationships they want to have and the kind of society they want to live in.

In the process it is important to remember that morality is 'embodied in the historical lives of particular social groups' and changes over time. Therefore:

> *morality which is no particular society's morality is to be found nowhere…Aristotle is the spokesman for one class of fourth century Athenians, Kant…provides a rational voice for the emerging social forces of liberal individualism…Nonetheless, if some particular moral scheme has successfully transcended the limitations of its predecessors to date and has then confronted successive challenges from a number of rival points of view, but in each case has been able*

*to modify itself in the ways required to incorporate the strengths of those points of view while avoiding their weaknesses and limitations **and** has provided the best explanation so far of those weaknesses and limitation, then we have the best possible reason to have confidence that future challenges will also be met successfully, that the principles that define the core of a moral scheme are enduring principles. And just this is the achievement that I ascribe to Aristotle's fundamental moral scheme.* (MacIntyre 1985:265-270)

Also:

Rationality itself, whether theoretical or practical, is a concept with a history: indeed, since there are a diversity of traditions of enquiry, with histories, there are, so it will turn out, rationalities rather than rationality, just as it will also turn out that there are justices rather than justice. (MacIntyre 1988:9)

As we struggle to grasp the various religious and philosophical perspectives and decide their relevance for youth work in our particular social and historical context, we are forced to confront Socrates' question 'how should one live?' – which is both singular and plural in the sense that it asks 'how should I live' as well as 'how should anyone live?' (Williams 1993:20)

The Buddha said:

Never believe any spiritual teaching because it is repeatedly recited; or because it is written down in the scriptures; or because it has been handed down from teacher to disciple; nor because everybody around you believes it; nor because it has metaphysical qualities; nor because it agrees with what you believe anyway; nor because you can rationalise it. Don't believe it if it is a viewpoint which you need to defend and don't believe it because the teacher is a reputable person or because the teacher said so...Don't believe something because it's a tradition, or because everybody around you does it, or because it's written in a book, but only, the Buddha said, if you have inquired into it and found it to be useful and true. (Khema 1987:160)

Part two
Practice

Youth work, as postulated in this book, engages young people in the process of moral philosophising as a function of their identity development and responsibility as social beings in a social world.

This does not mean having a fixed set of values or code of behaviour into which young people are to be initiated or inculcated. Philosophical pursuit necessarily involves reflection and questioning. Neither does it suggest that such an endeavour can be achieved primarily through engagement in structured exercises about imagined situations since the development of identity, the construction of the person, takes place not only through one's own agency but also through interaction with others. Indeed, as Shotter remarks, 'reality is constituted for us by the ways in which we render our activities accountable to one another in our daily social lives.' (Shotter quoted in Coleman and Hendry 1990:68)

> As what people say and do is always open to criticism and judgement by others, an essential part of being free individuals in a modern society, is them being able to justify their actions to others when required to do so – they require a capacity to be able to articulate 'good reasons' for their conduct. For, in executing their own actions, in acting as free agents (and in qualifying for their status as such), people cannot just act as they please, when they please. They must also act with a certain kind of socially shared awareness... (Shotter 1993:162)

The development of identity is not an insular activity. Therefore, in order to engage with young people, youth workers must make **relationships** with young people which enable them to develop the critical skills and moral dispositions needed to engage in the youth work **process**. A process which helps young people to make sense of themselves and their experiences and, in so doing, give meaning to their lives.

Relationships which involve:

- accepting and valuing young people
- honesty, trust, respect and reciprocity

And a process which involves young people in:

- **Learning** the skills of critical thinking and rational judgement.
- **Participating** in deliberations about what is 'good' – not only in particular respects but in terms of what is conducive to the good life generally. (Aristotle 1987)
- Taking charge of their lives as **empowered** individuals as opposed to powerless victims. That is as rational human beings able to 'understand and act on the personal, social and political issues which affect their lives, the lives of others and the communities of which they are a part.' (NYB 1991:16)

Central to the youth work process is a commitment to supporting young people to learn from their experience and 'make sense' of their lives through 'conversation' (Jeffs and Smith 1996) since 'talk, in the form of narratives, stories, accounts and so on, interprets what actions mean and thereby performs an evaluative function (Marshak 1998:21). And also because it is through narrative that 'people organise their experience in, knowledge about, and transactions with, the social world.' (Bruner quoted in Cortazzi 1993:1)

Relationships

The relationship is everything because personal growth, development, learning about values, are human tasks that can only be done within a relationship. Actually, the relationship is not only a base for sharing values but also the environment within which young people construct their sense of self – a model of themselves if you like, that they re-form and re-shape as they further explore and develop. Specifically, in the Christian context, the whole idea of an incarnate God is a central theme which speaks of 'being with' and 'sharing with' as a means by which people test the validity and accuracy of their values.

So youth work provides opportunities in safe environments for young people to challenge and be challenged in order to learn about themselves, their relationship to their immediate community, their relationship to the world and their relationship to their God.

Youth workers must, therefore, be able to initiate and develop relationships of trust and mutual respect with young people which motivate them to understand and develop their values. At the same time, young people need to feel safe enough to be open to sharing what they think and feel in order to enter into that sort of relationship. Of course, this all takes time. Values

cont...

are deeply personal, so the worker needs to keep focused on the young person and not be side-tracked by the benefits that they may see for some other party, be it the church or society in general.

(Neal Terry)

Relationships are, and always have been, at the heart of youth work. As such, it represents one of the most consistent themes in workers' accounts and other descriptions of the work. Relationships are important because it is within the context of 'being with' and 'sharing with' others that people are supported to create and re-create themselves, take charge of their relationships (with self and others), actively engage in their community and contribute to the world. This requires trust, mutual respect, safety and time.

> *The relationship between the youth worker and young person is like the foundation of a house. If it's not firmly established then the walls and ceiling will collapse. There is a responsibility on the youth worker to demonstrate to young people that positive relationships with adults are possible. They also need to use opportunities to be positive role models for young people and put a human face on the values that youth work is based on.*

> *We talk about all sorts of methods for empowering young people and even how to consult with them. But actually, it's the relationship that youth workers make with young people that forms the basis for young people's development and empowerment. It's the relationship that drives the process forward. That one-to-one relationship outweighs everything else. It's the foundation on which everything else is built.*

> *If you ask young people what they value about the youth service, they say the relationships with the staff. They always say that. They will give examples of being able to talk to workers about their family, school, relationships with other people and they may say, if I want to, they'll take me camping. I don't think that really happens in their contact with other agencies. Not in any consistent way.*

> *Youth workers are role models for the young people here. And, given the nature of this organisation as a Jewish youth and community centre, part of our work is about fostering environments that create positive Jewish identities for young people. It's about offering role models who themselves have those positive Jewish identities and people who can facilitate young people in exploring their own identities. It's about them being creative and exciting people and having a sense that the people who are working with them are also part of the community.*

However, whilst the relationship between the youth worker and young person has been a constant theme throughout the development of youth work, it is:

> the most elusive of all aspects...the worker cannot quantify this relationship to those 'outside' and yet, because of this, the worker is left to attempt to assess youth work in terms of the demands of those 'outside'. The failure of youth work has been its own reluctance to argue for a validity of a view from the 'inside'. Indeed, most accounts of practice focus upon the activity, assessing the work with young people in terms of 'doing' rather than 'being'. (Richardson 1997:91)

From activities to relationships

The truth, of course, is that most young people get involved in youth work because they are attracted by the activities on offer. They do not come for the relationship about which they possibly have no inkling, and they do not come for the 'social education' which we, as a service, hold so dear. They come for the activities and the facilities and the chance to do something – it does not even have to be that different. Sometimes they simply need a warm and welcoming place to be with friends.

> A number of years ago there was a questionnaire of young people in the rural villages. What the report said was that young people had nothing to do – which is absolutely true. There is a real problem with access to facilities. So when you ask young people around here what they want to do they say 'go to the Dome in Doncaster', which is a place where they can take part in almost any activity you can think of. They don't say they want 'social education' or a 'good listening ear from a youth worker'. After they've started to get involved in youth work they begin to recognise that there is something to be gained from engaging in a relationship with the youth worker which actually offers them more than they thought, because they thought they were just going to get to go canoeing or climbing or whatever. Here is something else that they didn't know about and were therefore unable to anticipate. So two things happen. Firstly, they recognise the relationship, and secondly, they come to value it.

> It was a summer's day and these two old gentlemen started walking towards us. At first, we thought it was someone's father but when he (the worker) came up he had these bright yellow A5 leaflets and he introduced himself, started telling us about some new project that was starting up and invited us to the youth project to have a chat. We were a bit apprehensive because you only really trust your own age group. Anybody older is basically outside it. So we started cracking a few jokes to break the ice and he started telling us what they were planning to do. And it seemed like it was basically giving us some power to do things for ourselves, like residentials and activities and so on. So we went along. But, in all honesty, it was basically for what we could get out of it for ourselves. That's what it came down to. But from there on it developed into a relationship – with trust.

When it first started off we just thought, well if they want to do this for us that's fair enough. We weren't doing anything apart from playing football in the park and going down the arcade. So we thought, great. Free residentials, activities, things we'd never had the opportunity to do before. But then most of us became aware that there was more to it than met the eye. It was about social development, acquiring new skills for yourself rather than just gallivanting off to whatever residential and doing activities. It gave us the abilities and skills to organise activities for ourselves. Which meant that we would later be able to say we did this or organised that. You had a certain idea about how to do things. Basically it made us look inside ourselves and say 'What am I doing here?' 'Where do I want to progress to in my life?' We also started looking at the neighbourhood and crime and thinking about what could be done about it. It was more or less a stepping stone for us to begin helping the community and in that way it encouraged more young people to join in the youth project.

Initially, young people may be attracted by the opportunity to take part in activities. They may decide to go along with things to see what they can get out of it for themselves – grasping the chance for a free weekend away or involvement in activities like 'canoeing or camping or whatever.' Pretty soon, however, they realise that there is more to this youth work than they first thought. They acquire and develop new skills and abilities. They look inside themselves and ask 'what am I doing here?' and 'where do I want to progress to in my life?'. They look at their neighbourhood and discover ways of helping the community.

Central to this experience is the relationship 'of trust' which young people come to recognise and value. Trust, then, is crucial. But what other features help to determine the nature of the relationship between youth workers and young people?

First of all, the relationship is voluntary and focused on young people.

The voluntary relationship is crucial. Young people don't choose their parents, or choose to go to school. They choose to be here.

The relationship needs to be based on young people's agenda and not on the worker's agenda. So, when they have an issue, they go and talk to the youth worker and it's their issue. The worker is not trying to get them through the national curriculum.

Indeed, Jeffs and Smith (1998), argue that one of the distinguishing characteristics of youth work is a voluntary relationship between the 'client or participant' and the worker, 'with the former invariably retaining the right to both initiate any association with the worker and more importantly to terminate it.' (1998:48)

The relationship between youth worker and young person is also underpinned by a collection of essential principles identified by workers and young people here as:

- accepting and valuing young people
- honesty

- trust
- respect
- reciprocity

Clearly, these are overlapping qualities. Acceptance, honesty, trust, respect and reciprocity are not separate entities. They combine together to create the broad foundation of the relationship within which the youth worker and young person explore and negotiate their own parameters. However, in taking a 'view from the inside', it is possible to identify and illustrate how youth work **practice** gives meaning to such concepts.

Accepting and valuing young people

If you are working with people, you have to understand that a person is about emotions, feelings, values, things that happened to them years before you got there and the experiences they've had. Youth work is about protecting that, honouring it, valuing that person for who they are and recognising that we have inequalities in society that affect people's lives. Youth work is about acknowledging those differences and not pretending that we are all equal or just making sure that particular individuals can do certain things.

You need to be honest about where they are at and where you're coming from. It's about not being judgmental. That probably sounds like a cliché but, particularly as an Asian woman worker, I'm really conscious that, if I'm working with young Asian women, it's crucial that they very quickly realise that I'm not the sort of person who's going to judge them. Many of the things that happen in their lives are to do with the communities from which they come and to which I also belong, so it's very important that they actually see that I'd be non-judgmental and also maintain confidentiality about whatever it is they share with me. The important thing is for them to know that I will not judge them, despite being a Hindu woman with the values and cultural norms that I come with.

I think youth work is about valuing people. The workers have really valued me and what I believe in and who I am, even though they don't always understand what I'm trying to do. They realise how important it is to me and so they're prepared to give me time and support.

Acceptance means accepting young people with all the emotions, feelings, values and history they come with. It means not judging young people whatever our cultural norms and values; and it means recognising how inequalities affect people's lives and seeking to challenge those inequalities, as opposed to simply securing opportunities for particular individuals. Acceptance means valuing young people – giving them time and support even when we may not fully understand what they are striving to achieve. Acceptance involves honesty.

Honesty

I think youth workers should be completely honest and open with young people about who you are and what you are capable of, what you can or cannot do with them. There are times when young people think that you can do a lot more than you can. At those moments there's often a temptation to go along with it because you think if we can get them in we can get the numbers up and so on. But actually that's not what it's about.

The principles of trust and honesty are central to youth work. I need to trust young people as much as they need to trust me. But it's always me that has to be the first one to take that risk of putting trust in them. They have to feel that I trust them. I also have to be honest and not have hidden agendas with them. If I'm about to do something about which they should be consulted, then I should consult them in an open and honest way. That's just showing respect, which is another important principle. Respecting them, their opinions, their talents and treating them as valued human beings.

The relationship between the youth worker and young person requires the worker to be honest and open about who they are, what they are capable of and what they have to offer. There is no hidden agenda in the youth work relationship. Workers consult with young people and 'put trust in them' – often being the first one to take that risk. Youth workers respect young people, their opinions, talents and treat them as valued human beings.

Respect

A youth worker does not have an automatic right to engage with a young person. I cannot assume that, just because I am an adult, that the young person wants to communicate with me. Therefore, the establishment of a relationship that is based on respect and trust is absolutely crucial. Besides, young people can always see through charades, through people who are patronising, people who are tokenistic, people who hide behind their authority.

It's about recognising that the situation a young person may be in is their situation. So we don't take a situation that the young person is in away from them, muck about with it and give it back to them and say 'what do you think?' We keep them involved the whole time.

People need to feel connected to each other. Young people will only hear you if they have a level of respect for you and, obviously, if you are open and genuine, but also if they can see that you do actually care about them. And if you don't actually care about them, young people pick that up very quickly. In fact, some youth workers may even talk about a level of love for the young people that they work with – which means having positive regard for them. Viewing them as positive beings and being able to offer them support on their terms.

Respect in the relationship means recognising that youth workers do not have an automatic right to intervene in young people's lives or even to engage with them. Relationships are negotiated with trust and respect, and within an understanding that young people's lives, situations and issues belong to them. Respect means having a positive regard for young people, genuinely caring about them and being prepared to support them on **their** terms.

Trust

> To me, young people are no different from adults in the sense that they only share their hopes and fears with people they trust. Like adults, they are more likely to listen to and consider the views of somebody who they feel has their best interest at heart even if they are saying difficult things. That's very different from feeling that people are either trying to manipulate you or that they just don't care. So, if workers are going to challenge young people about their behaviour or question the choices they make, then that's only going to be accepted by young people if they feel there is some trust and respect in that relationship.

> I'm quite honest with young people in terms of what I'm thinking about what they are saying and what they are doing. But if they listen to me it's because of the respect and trust that's built up between them and me, not because I'm an adult in authority and therefore I'm right.

> I am a volunteer leader now but I used to be a member at the centre and what I can remember I saw was trust and leaders who had patience and time, who were bothered to want to help. With that kind of person you made a bond – someone that understands you and shows patience and time and trust, and someone that just cares really. I think that's one of the most important things in youth work. You've got to really care about what you are doing because, if you don't, then there's no real point in doing what you're doing.

Young people, like all other people, share their hopes and fears with people they trust. They are also prepared to consider the opinion of people they trust even if those opinions are difficult to take on. But what makes a person trustworthy? The main message seems to be – 'you can trust people who care', people who take the time and show the patience and who are bothered enough to want to help.

> The bottom line is trust, respect and honesty, and believing that young people have got the ability to change and to grow and to be whatever they want to be, as long as they've got enough support in their lives.

> Youth workers are trustworthy in the sense that you can tell them stuff and also if I needed someone they'd be there for me…(the worker) is completely on my level – which is funny because, before I got involved in youth work, I didn't really think much of youth workers, I just thought they were prats. And then after a while I thought, God, they earn so much respect and you really don't appreciate them.

Reciprocity

There is a sense that the relationship is two-way. Youth workers support young people knowing that young people also have skills, valid perspectives and expertise of their own. Young people also have something to offer, not only in practical ways…

> If I go ice skating with young people they need to help me because I can't skate to save my life. But that's good because, as youth workers, we don't claim to be experts at everything. In fact, sometimes we need the young people's expertise which is good for them as much as for us.

But in terms of 'being there', their sensitivity and concern…

> I try to be sensitive to young people's needs. I don't build their hopes and then disappear. The young people I'm working with know I'll be there when I'm needed so there's a much deeper kind of relationship between us. They have my home telephone number. I don't give it to all the young people. I choose who I give it to and it's those who I know won't abuse it. They'll use it when they need it and that's fine. Some also have my address at home and a few have visited me at home. Not necessarily because of any particular reason but just because they wanted to. They just felt like it. So they'll ring up and then come over. When they come to my house I make them welcome because I don't live in the area where I work and I acknowledge the effort they've made in travelling to see me – just because they wanted to see how I was. That's a reward that I find fascinating because it motivates me. You know we all work for money. If we didn't get money, OK we might do a few hours of voluntary work but not full-time like this. You've got the mortgage to pay or whatever. But the financial side doesn't cheer me up. I think generally it doesn't cheer people up. It's the people you're working with. They are the ones who motivate you. So one of the things that I've always thought important in youth work is that you're not doing it for the money. You're doing it because you feel for young people. You have to feel their experience and what they're going through to actually do youth work. And you have to acknowledge it. Whether it's a positive or negative experience, you have to feel for them and their needs in that situation. That's how they motivate you and you motivate them. It's done in partnership. Youth work is not a one-way process. It's not like I'm the youth worker and I'm expert at these issues and this is how it is. No. Young people have something to offer as well.

> Youth workers are like family. You know, someone who'll always be there. That's how I take them. You can let your guard down with them because they let theirs down with you. It's a two-way system. You give. They give. You respect them. They respect you.

The youth worker as mentor

Interestingly, Philip and Hendry's (1996) study of young people and mentoring, highlighted the qualities of 'helping relationships' as including honesty, respect, acceptance, (adult) interest in young people, trust (particularly in relation to confidentiality), empathy and elements of reciprocity, adults who are open to negotiation, and adults who are less authoritarian. Actually, the very same qualities identified here in relation to youth workers relationships with young people.

However, Philip and Hendry's study did not work from the more traditional definition of mentoring – that is, a one-to-one relationship with someone more experienced and usually older within which the young person is supported and challenged, thereby enhancing the 'transition from adolescence to adulthood' (Philip and Hendry 1996:189). Instead, they worked from the position of asking young people to identify instances in which they had **felt** supported and challenged by individuals and/or groups. (1996:190) The result was the identification of five 'forms of mentoring' – one-to-one; individual to group (e.g. as in the youth work setting); friend to friend; peer group; and long term one-to-one.

Whilst understanding about the nature of mentoring is changing, (Russell and Adams 1997; Eby 1997) there is still a question to be asked about what, if anything, distinguishes mentoring from other forms of 'helping relationships' and, in particular, the relationship between youth worker and young person.

Three features would seem particularly significant here. Firstly, the importance of 'long-term relationships where trust was assured and negotiation was possible' as stressed by the young people involved in the Philip and Hendry study (1996:199). One cannot therefore conceive of mentoring as a kind of 'one off' occasion. Mentoring takes place within the context of a relationship which is very often informal in nature (Philip and Hendry 1996). Indeed, Noe (1988) notes that the majority of mentoring relationships (in organisations) are informal:

> *That is, the relationship develops because of shared interest, admiration, or job demands that require the skills of two or more persons. In informal mentoring relationships, discussions between the mentor and protégé usually go beyond career-related issues to more in-depth personal sharing of interests, needs and values.* (Noe 1988:458)

This issue of formality/informality therefore represents the second significant feature of 'mentoring' relationships. In formal organisational 'mentoring' relationships, a mentor (usually a senior, more experienced employee) is assigned to support a younger employee through acting as a role model, providing support, direction and feedback' (Noe 1988). Similarly, recent 'mentoring' schemes in work with young people have been based on the assignment of mentors – be they independent volunteers specifically recruited and trained (Burke and Loewenstein 1998), or within careers service work, adults in employment or careers service advisers (ECOTEC 1997). 'Mentoring' is, then, the expressed purpose of the relationship as opposed to 'mentoring' taking place within the context of an on-going relationship.

This leads to the third significant feature – the question of purpose. In the business world, the purpose of mentoring schemes is to support the interpersonal development and career opportunities of the younger employee. In relation to work with young people, the 'mentoring' approach is being developed largely in the area of work with young people 'at risk', where the work is seen very much in terms of influencing the behaviour of young people – for example, in relation to offending, drug use or truancy. (NYA 1997b) Similar objectives exist in careers service work with 'disaffected' young people, which focuses on job support and career search initiatives, re-entry to education and training, jobs and qualification. (ECOTEC 1997)

Such an approach sits in direct contradiction to the experiences of the young people in the Philip and Hendry (1996) study, for whom 'helping relationships' created space, time and support for **their** interests, needs and issues and finding solutions to **their** questions. That is, of course, very different from an imposed agenda arising, not out of young people's concerns, but out of the concerns of others. So while:

> Mentoring provides protégés with the opportunity to develop skills, gain access to developmental opportunities, build the confidence necessary to tackle challenging tasks, and obtain guidance and counselling (Kram 1985 cited in Eby 1997:126)

mentoring works best when:

> the need is the 'acquisition of wisdom'. By wisdom we mean here the ability to relate what has been learned to a wide spectrum of situations, and to achieve 'insight' and 'understanding' into the issues discussed. (Clutterbuck and Sweeney 1997:3)

Clearly, a formal and focused approach to mentoring has the distinct advantage of ensuring equality of access to opportunities for support, guidance and career advancement for particular groups of people – e.g. women, Black people. However, it has also been acknowledged that:

> assigned mentoring relationships may not be as beneficial as mentoring relationships that develop informally, due to personality conflicts between parties...and the lack of true personal commitment of either the mentor or the protégé to the relationship because it was not formed on their initiative. (Noe 1988:458)

The upshot is that mentoring is most effective when:

- it takes place within the context of an on-going relationship
- it is informally initiated by the parties involved
- it pursues the acquisition of wisdom
- all parties make a personal commitment to the process

Youth workers are, therefore, invariably involved in the **activity** of mentoring in the sense that they engage in informally initiated relationships with young people within which young people are supported and challenged to gain greater insight and understanding of themselves, their relationships and their world; and to which there is a deliberate commitment. This may take the form of the kind of one-to-one relationships, individual to group relationships or long term one-to-one relationships which Philip and Hendry identify. (1996)

However, youth workers are not formal 'mentors' in the sense that:

- They are not assigned – the relationship is informal and, therefore, the nature and extent of 'guidance and challenge' is (informally) negotiated with young people.
- Their work with young people focuses not on the priorities and concerns of others, but on the interests, needs and concerns of young people themselves.

He…(the youth worker) has had more experience than us. He's been there. He's seen it. And he's advising us. He's not telling us like our parents do. At first we didn't really take any notice. We just thought yeah, yeah, yeah. But over the years he's said things to us and even if we didn't take any notice at the time they've come back to haunt us. So then you think about it and you go 'oh yeah, he was right'. And from that you say 'all right, let's see what he's got to say'.

I met…(the worker) two years ago when I was 15 and trying to set up a self-help mental health project for young people who suffer from distress. At that time I think I was sort of having a breakdown but when I met…(the worker), I was sort of coming through it. She was very open to new ideas and was very accepting. With her support I've now set up the group and won a Millennium Award so I've got funding for a year and I'm based at the Council House. But at the time I didn't really understand what her role was as a youth and community worker because I'd never even heard of youth and community workers before. So we had to work out what the relationship was and how she could best guide and advise me. That's not been easy because the workers have been very unsure and even frightened at times. But they thought here is a young person who is passionate about what she wants to do, let's support her even if at times they didn't understand the issues involved.

The most important thing about the relationship is that it creates the environment for young people to explore their questions and answers in a genuine and meaningful way. Conversations with young people begin with 'how are you?' not 'what's your issue?'

But even this does not adequately describe the relationship between a youth worker and young person. For, in addition to the 'helping' qualities outlined above (acceptance, honesty, trust, respect, reciprocity), there is an added, more intangible quality that can only be truly understood by way of comparison. In other words, by comparing the youth work relationship with some other relationship with which young people are familiar. For many young people that comparison is made in the form of a 'friend'. A youth worker is seen as being **like** a friend.

What is interesting is that, while youth workers themselves tend to see this as problematic and are disinclined to describe the relationship as a kind of 'friendship', young people are often only too clear about the lines of demarcation. For them, youth workers are like 'friends' at the same time as also being not like 'friends'.

The youth worker as 'friend'

It's important that you get on with the youth workers because if you don't then there's not much point coming here. The relationship is like a friendship but it won't be such a strong friendship, just a mutual friendship where you respect them and they respect you. You can talk to them about anything really. Sometimes you may want to talk to a youth worker about things you are thinking about. Sometimes I may go to my friends. What makes youth workers different is that they are not controlling you. You come here because you want to, whereas with school you go there because you have to. So because you come here because you want to, it's a lot more friendly and you have a laugh.

Youth workers are sort of almost my friends. In fact, more than that. I can trust them with stuff I wouldn't tell my friends because I would be afraid that my friends might freak out and have a panic reaction. Like, for example, when you first tell a friend that you are gay, if they've never met a gay person they might freak. But with youth workers you can tell them anything. They have some idea about how to deal with it. They can be supportive. Even if they don't agree with it, they're not judgmental. Unless it's about drugs and things like that. Then they can be quite judgmental. They'll never march up to you and say 'what you're doing is wrong, stop it now'. But they have their own ways of telling you that maybe it isn't such a good idea.

A youth worker is like a friend because they see you grow up and they are always there. They know your family. They're there when you are in trouble. They know all about your life so they're sort of always in the background or in the foreground. It's like having a big sister or big auntie who you can tell things that you wouldn't tell anyone else. I know some people have sisters and aunties like that but if you don't it's good to have a youth worker around. But youth workers are not your friend because you are not part of their social life. You are part of their work life.

Because youth work is mainly in the evening, you can sometimes think it's social time and that you're friends with the youth workers. But you're not, so it can be frustrating. What you have to realise is that the youth worker's relationship with you is work. When I became a volunteer youth worker myself, I understood it much more clearly. Like, there are some of the girls in my group who I really like and would be friends with but, because their parents know me as the worker I can't go out with them on a personal level because I would always be responsible. Like, if I went to a club or something then the parents would think, 'why are you taking my daughter to a club, is that part of your job description?' So you have to keep a clear boundary.

Youth workers are like 'friends' in the sense that there is mutual respect, young people talk with workers about 'anything', workers are not judgmental, they understand young people's issues and pressures, young people choose to engage in the relationship, workers are not controlling and young people can 'have a laugh' with them.

Youth workers are not like 'friends' because young people are not a part of their social life. Young people sometimes tell workers things they would not tell their friends. Youth workers are more like family, an aunt or sister, who are always there. Youth workers have more experience and knowledge than peers. Youth workers maintain clear boundaries.

From the worker's point of view:

> *I am not their friend. I am there as a youth worker but I like to feel that the approach is friendly and that they can approach me and we can have a discussion and talk things through. In the process, I can and will challenge their comments, behaviour or attitudes and hopefully we can talk about that because they know I'm not coming with some kind of authoritarian attitude. That the relationship is more informal, more flexible. Sometimes I'll get angry and sometimes they'll be angry with me. But at the end of the session it will be like 'see you next week' because it's over and finished. Or it may not be. It may continue. But the important thing is that I get across to that young person that I still value them. I still support them and I still care about them as a person. I just don't care about some of their beliefs or attitudes and I make that difference perfectly clear.*

Subscribing to the idea of the youth worker as 'friend' is problematic since the word carries heavy associations of 'socialising' which detract from the essential 'professional' or 'work focus' intended. Many workers, therefore, balk at the suggestion, while young people seem much more able to draw a distinction between 'a friend' (i.e. peer) and someone who is 'like a friend' (a youth worker).

However, taking Aristotle's lead, it becomes possible to understand the concept of a friend as 'someone who likes and is liked by another person', given that 'liking' is defined as:

> *wanting for someone what one thinks good for his* [sic] *sake and not for one's own, and being inclined, so far as one can, to do such things for him...out of concern for him and not, or not merely, out of concern for oneself.* (Cooper 1980:302)

But how do youth workers show this concern for young people?

Empathy

> *One of our best part-time workers came here originally as a Prince's Trust Volunteer. Six years later he is a qualified youth worker who may well get the other full-time post here. One of*

the key things about his relationships with the young people is that he comes from the immediate area. He started where lots of the young people are. He didn't fly in from middle class suburbia with all the qualifications and so on. He struggled to become qualified. And, because he comes from this neighbourhood, then it's easy for the young people to identify with him. He can empathise with their situation. He's been where they are. He can understand what they are going through as white working class kids living in this neighbourhood. They trust him and they want to talk with him about things that matter to them.

The relationship is essentially empathetic. It is about seeing young people and young people feeling they have been seen. They have been recognised in some way, which is a kind of spiritual thing that's about self and a very fundamental recognition of one human by another in a very focused way. That's not an easy thing to do. And it's more difficult when you are busy. But I think it happens more often than not since the young people here are not simply seen as a mass to be serviced.

Listening to young people

When I came here, there was a leader who loved football and I got on really well with him and, even though I wasn't the best behaved kid, I felt I could trust him. He was understanding, and just listened and gave me attention. Teachers are doing their job; they don't care about your feelings. They don't listen. They just say 'Oh you've got homework or whatever'. But here it's more like a community. It's nice.

The way youth workers connect with young people is crucial. That means giving a clear message that I am listening to you and you alone right now. Showing respect for young people's space – none of this head patting – metaphorically or physically – or 'Come to me, I'm a youth worker and you're my job'.

Taking account of young people's views and ideas

The club is for young people with learning disabilities. When I first started there, we didn't have members meetings. The workers decided what the young people wanted within the club programme and we decided how it was going to be run. I then started the members' meetings and got a lot of hostility from some of the volunteers who said things like 'Well, they'll never sit still for a start, never mind getting them to talk about what they want or how to build a programme.' So I had to get over that to start with and sometimes it was a case of even saying to some of the volunteers 'I'd rather, if you're not going to take an active part in this and disrupt it by shuffling, moving, getting up, then I'd rather you just stayed out of the room'. So it took a long slow process to get the young people to actually say what they wanted and engage in a process of negotiation about what was possible. From that experience they started to realise that we were going to listen to them. So we were building up a relationship where they came to trust us more and more. They then started to tell us about what had gone on at school or what some of their personal fears were, how they were feeling, peer pressure, what some of their girlfriend or boyfriend issues were. It was a gradual process of building that relationship and responding to them with compassion, which made them more willing to discuss things about themselves and their lives.

I think a young person ought to be able to come and talk to you about their experiences, their life, their problems. And you should be able to support that young person and help them through some of those issues and problems. You should also have a relationship where the young person is part of the youth work programme in terms of having an input into what goes on at the centre or project. You're working with young people not working for them.

The key thing is the relationship that youth workers have with young people. That relationship is about young people being able to open up and talk to us. They come in because they want to come in. They want to participate. They want to take part. If you look at schooling, social work – it's young people being told that they have to do it. But in youth work it's about what young people want to do. It's about getting their ideas. Getting their views. And using their ideas and views to take them forward.

Helping young people to 'see' themselves

Before I met…(the worker), I'd never had any contact with anyone else who I could talk to about my problems or experiences and who could actually help me to realise what I thought and make my own decisions. He doesn't tell us. He asks us and he gives his own viewpoint, just his viewpoint, rather than saying this is what you should do, he says this is what you could do. And that's a completely different way of saying something. Different from other adults. Also, he was on the same wavelength. He understood our language. Teachers were more formal. They used to speak more formally to us. So I felt more comfortable talking to…(the worker) because I see him more as a friend whereas, if I was talking to a teacher, I wouldn't feel comfortable and there are things I wouldn't tell the teacher.

The relationship between youth worker and young person enables us to look below the superficial and explore opportunities for reflection. That's not to say that when you look at me you see yourself, but that there is some kind of openness and willingness to be available on young people's terms. What you see is me reflecting you back to yourself. What you don't see is me, my ego, my problems, my issues, my worries, my experience of what you're going through. You will see yourself. That's the ideal. So this is more than just a mirror that reflects back and has no personality. It's about being there for the other person, as a role model that young people aspire to be whether it is because of wanting to be as thoughtful as the worker, as reflective, or sensitive or willing to listen.

The youth worker as role model

People model themselves on others through a process of observing others' actions and the consequences of others' actions, and adjusting their own behaviour. It is something we learn at an early age. Indeed, Bandura (1974) observed that this is the very process which children use to learn language. Children observe the effects of different sequences of sound and words and imitate them. Some reproductions are verbatim. However, on many other occasions children reconstruct their observations to create sentences they have never actually heard. In so doing, they move beyond mere imitation to grasp the ability to produce appropriate responses to new situations.

It is not just language that people learn in this way. The process of imitation and reconstruction accounts for many of the life skills that constitute our daily experience. For the most part, such learning happens on a subconscious level. However, while this natural learning process has been developed into a highly structured learning technique (behaviour role modelling – Bandura 1974), the informal nature of youth work means that 'role modelling' is likely to remain somewhat ethereal. Yet, we often describe youth workers as role models for young people. But what do we mean?

Our project is about working with young people involved in or on the margins of the drug culture. But actually, the most important thing is not about giving them information or going in heavy about drugs. It's about making meaningful and constructive relationships with young people. That's the key. And in order to do that, you need consistency and continuity. You can't parachute into this kind of work.

Offering a positive role model is crucial. That means being clear and explicit about your own values. Saying what you stand for. Drawing firm lines. And setting high standards for yourself and young people. Young people are not stupid. They know what is right and wrong and they believe in fairness. What they want to know is what you are about.

Trust and credibility are not there for the asking. It's about being real and consistent. We have to do the right thing in the way we behave and interact and lead our lives. People see us every day walking down the street or out shopping or whatever. We can't afford to be hypocritical, because the success of this project rests on our integrity as people as much as our integrity as workers.

cont...

We work from a Black perspective, which means five things to us. Firstly, recognising that we live in an inherently racist society and understanding race, racism and oppression as being socially constructed. We also think it is crucial to have an understanding of Black culture and history. Valuing education is important because knowledge is power but, actually, knowing how to use knowledge is more powerful. The Black perspective is also about doing something. Taking action and being positive about what you are going to do. Finally, it's about building on tradition and continuity and recognising the rich and lengthy tradition of youth work in this community which will continue long after the end of this particular project.

(Michael Clarke and Paul Mattis)

The idea of the youth worker as role model is, therefore, grounded in the necessity for workers to practise what they preach – to establish the 'moral authority' (Jeffs and Smith 1996), which underpins their integrity as people and gives credibility to their work as practitioners. It is not, therefore, so much a case of imitation, but establishing the value base or ethical framework within which the relationship and youth work itself operates. In other words, letting young people know 'what you are about' and living true to it.

> *An inevitable consequence of the voluntary nature of the relationship between young people and youth workers is that the latter, perhaps more than other educators, rely on their moral authority to secure a constituency. Securing and retaining such authority, often in trying circumstances, creates an ever present tension within the work for, without resorting to subterfuge, they must seek to become the kind of people that young people 'can trust, both intellectually and with regard to their character...steady, completely reliable and consistent* (Warnock 1993, quoted in Jeffs and Smith 1999:71)

But the importance of the worker's 'moral authority' is about much more than merely 'securing a constituency', since the very intention of youth work is to engage young people in a process of examining and exploring values and morals. As one worker remarks:

> *We say that youth work is about informal and social education, but I think it is actually about more than that. It's an education, that is grounded in young people's active search to discover what they think and how they feel and where their values match up with their sense of who they are.*

Engagement in such self exploration cannot, therefore, be undertaken simply as a matter of developing the 'cognitive equipment needed for autonomous moral judgement'. For youth work, like moral education, is not 'just or mostly a matter of moral reasoning, but a growth in our concern for what we are in our relationships with each other' (Kleinig 1982:252).

Therefore, the role model offered by youth workers not only establishes their 'moral authority', but also, and importantly, creates the ethical framework for their relationships with young people and secures the basis for engagement in the process of moral philosophising which youth work necessarily involves.

> *Adults can seem like very scary figures sometimes but youth workers are usually down to earth characters. You can just sit down and chat with them about anything and everything for hours. It's really a lot of fun. Actually I'm baffled by the relationship. It's not like a social worker and a client relationship. It's more flexible. It's different. It's not like a parent and child. It's not like a teacher. Not like going to the doctors. It's not like anything. It's not like having a friend. It's like youth workers are none of these things but all of them rolled into one. So they need a kind of personality that's open to everything and the ability to talk to anybody and everybody. You need to be able to have a laugh with them. And if you think about...(the worker) you can see that she genuinely cares about people.*

Process

Youth work is educational and therefore, following Dewey, it is not an activity for inculcating rigid patterns of socially accepted behaviour. It is not a static yardstick but a set of processes which must be reassessed to meet the needs of different individuals, situations and circumstances. Also, education is its own end – a liberating experience which encourages reflective behaviour and promotes growth and health; developing the individual and supporting their participation in society. (Dewey1961) As such, youth work's intention is to liberate, as opposed to domesticate, young people. (Freire 1972). Indeed, education as the practice of freedom enables people to:

> *reflect on themselves, their responsibilities, and their role in the new cultural climate – indeed to reflect on the very power of reflection. The resulting development of this 'power' [being] an increased capacity for choice.* (Freire 1976:16)

Once you've established some trust, a good way to begin is to give young people some responsibility. Running the café is a good example. It offers the chance for involvement and ownership. It's true that sometimes we've made a wrong judgement in giving out such responsibilities. Maybe the young person wasn't ready for it. Maybe they were so much in poverty that it was like putting it on a plate for them. But we're not talking about phenomenal amounts of money so there's always been the opportunity to discuss the whole issue of morals. And that has led on to conversations about what it means to have taken from your own community and then looking at where that young person is, why are they doing that and what their needs are.

Within the social education context, a lot of the work is about enabling young people to explore and make choices, whether it's about leaving home or all the other issues that come up. So what we try to do is to create a curriculum that gives them opportunities to explore moral issues. That is political sometimes. So, in an agency like this, 'outing' is a regular discussion amongst young people. That enables us to tap into debates about the consequences of 'outing' – for example, loss of family, friends, job – and whether or not it is essential for people to be 'out and proud'.

We do a sort of 'problem page' session which we normally recycle about once a term. During this, people are able to write down problems for the agony aunt to resolve. Generally what happens is the agony aunt, who will be one of the young people in the group, tries to promote debate. Through that process the young people will have an opportunity to explore rights and wrongs. Sometimes the staff put things in to provoke discussion because they know of an issue or something that's going on. For example, a while ago we realised that quite a few of the young people were working on the 'rent scene'. And although we'd talked about some of the issues and run some sessions on self assertion, it didn't work very effectively. But when we started using structured sessions with case studies and scenarios, young people started to get more involved in the discussion and were more able to open up.

(Mo Hand)

The youth work process is, therefore, a reflective exercise which enables young people to:

- learn from their experience
- develop their capacity to think critically
- engage in 'sense-making' as a process of continuous self discovery and re-creation

Learning from experience

The learning process in youth work involves reflection and deliberation. So learning is not envisaged simply as a process of 'inert ideas…[being] received into the mind without being utilised, or tested, or thrown into fresh combinations' (Alfred North Whitehead quoted in Freire 1976:36). Learning is seen as a dynamic process which leads to action. In other words, to be meaningful, learning needs to be tested in reality.

Kolb's (1984) experiential learning cycle is a particularly helpful diagrammatic representation of this integrated reflection/action model of learning. As such, the learning process is described in four stages:

1. The young person's experience – whether arising from everyday life or some particular youth work opportunity.

2. The opportunity for the young person to reflect on the experience, analysing not only what he or she thinks but also how she or he feels.

3. The development of understanding through which the young person:
   - examines their thoughts and feelings about this experience in relation to other situations and experiences
   - gathers information from other sources (e.g. other young people, the youth worker, other adults, books, newspapers, videos, etc.)
   - integrates these reflections and information into a logical and rational framework for decision-making and future action.

4. The 'testing' of the young person's new 'theory' in a real life situation.

Of course, the learning does not end here. For 'testing in reality' gives rise to new experiences which, in turn, trigger a new learning cycle of reflection, understanding and testing in reality.

Also, the young person's 'experience' may not necessarily be something that 'happened'. It may be information they have received or ideas they have encountered. In any case, what the young person is faced with is a new 'situation' which, in order to derive learning, they must reflect on and come to some understanding which can inform their future thinking and action.

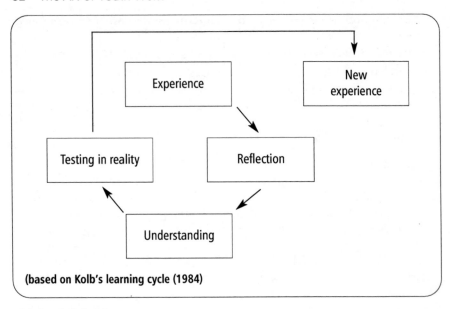

(based on Kolb's learning cycle (1984)

Critical thinking

Central to this process is the capacity to reason – the capacity to think critically. In other words, the capacity to:

- identify and challenge assumptions
- recognise the importance of the social, political and historical contexts of events, assumptions, interpretations and behaviour
- imagine and explore alternatives
- exercise reflective scepticism towards claims to universal truths or ultimate explanations (Brookfield 1987)

Critical thinking therefore entails the ability to:

- grasp the **meaning** of a statement
- avoid **ambiguity**
- spot **contradictions**
- judge what **follows**, what is **assumed**, and when a conclusion is *unwarranted*
- decide when a definition is **adequate**
- decide when an **observation, statement** or **authority** is reliable
- decide when a problem has been properly **identified** and adequately resolved (Ennis, 1962 cited in Fisher 1991:50)

This, of course, is no easy task. It requires discipline and practice. In fact, reasoning, according to Dewey (1900, *The School and Society*, cited in Whalley 1991), is sharpened and perfected through disciplined discussion. Therefore, the activity of 'discussion' becomes crucial to the youth work process. Indeed, according to Paulo Freire:

> The mark of a successful educator is not skill in persuasion – which is but an insidious form of propaganda – but the ability to dialogue with educatees in a mode of reciprocity.
> (Freire 1976:xiii)

Dialogue or 'conversation'

> The relationship that young people have with youth workers here is informal. Most of the interaction takes place through conversation, so the worker needs to be able to think very clearly about the conversations that go on with young people – what their role is or what kind of intervention they can make. To do that you need to have enough knowledge and foresight about what is likely to happen next and a readiness to use conversations as opportunities to be in the role of an educator, albeit informal. That's what makes conversations meaningful.

> Meaningful conversations don't just happen. You have to create an environment for them to take place. An atmosphere that has warmth, fun, spontaneity. An environment that enables young people to broaden their knowledge, understand the complexity of the issues they are involved in and express themselves in a clear, straight forward and assertive way. Once you have a relationship, that work can be over and done with in a matter of seconds. It makes another building block and maybe later on something else will happen and that young person will feel confident to come back to you for another conversation.

Green and Christian (1998) refer to 'accompanying' – a process which they liken to a pianist 'accompanying' a soloist. What is required is concentration and attention, and a striving to 'pick up the mood' of the soloist with sensitivity and awareness. 'Accompanying' means 'being alongside' young people. 'Being there'. (1998:20) It is:

> an empathetic conversation where one person supports another and enables them to explore the full range of emotions, thoughts and consequences of part of their life. Both the accompanied and accompanist have to listen to each other and are learning and growing from the conversation. However, the accompanist is giving the gift of a platform to the accompanied, who is then able to analyse, accept and make plans concerning their current situation. (Green and Christian 1998:23)

The qualities of 'accompanying' are identified as empathy, sympathy, tolerance, respect for the viewpoint of the accompanied, being grounded (or centred), personal space, life experience, understanding, wisdom, active listening, concentration and grace – awareness of the spirit moving in the lives of both the accompanied and accompanying person. (Green and Christian 1998:28)

Conversations in context

Conversations are, therefore, the bedrock on which youth work is built. But conversations do not happen in a vacuum. Conversations have contexts. For example, conversations sometimes occur in the process of offering 'personal support' to young people.

> *Before I met…(the worker) I wasn't really into education. If I failed an exam I would just give up. But he's given me the sense to just carry on and work even harder at it. He's shown me a different kind of view, if you like. And I've realised that if I get an education I've got a better chance of getting a job that I like instead of just working in a factory or something like that for the rest of my life. So if I hadn't met him I wouldn't be going to university. I would have probably found myself a job and started working on from there.*

Youth workers use conversations to help young people explore their 'options and choices'.

> *I view my role as ensuring that young people have an awareness that there are other options. For instance, if I'm talking to a young person who is doing their GCSEs and thinking about A levels, I might ask them 'what has your careers advisor advised, what are you interested in, what do you dream about doing?' Their answer is very much located around going to work in this society. So I may explore with them other options, such as developmental work in the Caribbean or another area of the developing world, volunteering for a black organisation, VSO or simply not feeling pressured to make a fixed decision at this point, looking further than what the agenda of capitalism has to offer.*

Youth workers engage in conversations within the context of offering 'challenging experiences' to young people.

> The value of the Duke of Edinburgh Award scheme is the structure, because it allows you to get into some good youth work very quickly rather than having to work your way through the initial stages in getting to know the young people and getting them involved. For example, in the expedition section young people get to do things that they wouldn't dream of doing otherwise. So, if you said to the young people in the youth club 'Do you

cont...

want to come away walking 15 miles for two days camping overnight and carrying all the stuff with you?' they'd laugh at you. But the structure of the Award is such that they are keen to do that for the challenge that is there in terms of completing the bronze award. On the final expedition they are on their own, but in all the build up to it you are walking or whatever with them and, as with any residential or outdoor work, there are golden opportunities to get to know those young people better. Also, if the weather is bad you are suffering alongside them. The staff here have never been into sitting in the minibus while the young people are walking along in the rain and wind. It's very much that we are doing it with them.

I think providing leadership opportunities is very important. So, for the service section of the Duke of Edinburgh's Award, we've got young people working, alongside the workers, as volunteers with the five to eight year olds. It's done very much in partnership so there's a sense in which the young people are treated just like the rest of the staff. That's good for their self-esteem and sense of self-worth. Also it means that we're able to show that we are human. Perhaps we are having problems with one particular child just like they are. What you get is a bonding between the volunteer and the worker. In fact, we now have about nine young people aged 16–19, who've been volunteers for two or three years, that we employ to work with the under 12s. It's an experience that's given them a lot in terms of their growth and personal development.

We also take an interest in outside qualifications like the Community Sports Leaders Award and, in fact, we have three young people, including one young woman, who are FA qualified coaches. Part of our strategy for this year actually includes looking for more opportunities to involve young people in courses leading to external qualifications. That's important because we think it helps young people to see that it's not just the workers here who think they have abilities and potential.

(Dave Stannard)

Sometimes youth workers utilise structured activities and situations to 'kick start' conversations that help young people to 'think about their lives, their experiences and their values'.

We ran a programme on decision making last year for the 16 plus age group. We asked them things like how they made decisions about how their bedroom was going to look, how they decided whether to smoke or not – which is a always a big thing on residentials. How they decided what their signature was going to look like for the rest of their life. What sort of process did they go through? How did they want their signature to represent them? What did they want it to say about them? They were stunned. The main thing that came out of the session was us asking the questions because the response was 'My God, no one has ever asked me such questions before and I've never thought about them.' And this is 16 to 19 year olds. After that it became possible to ask other questions like 'Why do you be like you are? How come you are like yourself? How come you did this and not that?' OK, these are big philosophical questions for teenagers but the significant thing is, they were so excited to be asked. During the course of the programme they became more reflective and more analytical. I think they responded differently to the programme because they suddenly got more excited about themselves. To explain themselves to someone else was really exciting for them. Not as an interrogation but from the point of view of saying 'I've thought about it and I have this opinion' which was a revelation to them. And the fact that someone had asked them these questions and was prepared to engage in discussion meant that they come through expecting to be negotiated with.

We use all sorts of activities to help young women think about and work out their values – like a problem page activity or something like that where you get the problem and each group has to write their answer. We use activities like that to help us think about what's right, while recognising that there's not necessarily one right answer. So, for example, there may be a value about respecting other people but there's not necessarily a right way of handling a situation. What's important is that young women get the chance to talk through the different ways you might handle a situation while recognising the important principles involved.

During the run up to the 1997 general election, a group of young people that I had been working with for about three years started to ask questions about what was going on in the media and about the various parties and individuals involved. Several of the group were voting for the first time and therefore wanted to discuss who they should vote for as young Christians. What we decided to do was to get a better understanding by gathering information about the three main parties and visiting the local government offices. We then went on to organise and run a six-nation youth camp to compare and contrast systems and look at how we participate in Europe. The camp also included input from a Christian socialist. Through the process, the young people got a chance to meet MPs and MEPs. No particular decisions were made as to who they would vote for but the young people did come away with a clear sense of the importance of their participation in the democratic process and they did engage in some deep and wide ranging discussions about the value bases of the various parties.

We have a programme, developed jointly with the local adventure playground, that involves work with 10-14 year olds in four local primary schools. It's a structured series of weekly sessions based on ten key principles called 'Do The Right Thing'.

1. Treat others as you would like to be treated.

2. Listen and you will be heard.

3. Do not shout at, just speak to others.

4. Positive attracts positive.

5. Achieving is believing and believing is achieving.

6. Each one teach one.

7 Set your own standards, live by example.

8. Share and care for your own space.

9. Speak with your mouth not with your fists.

10. Wake up to your faults and do something about it.

Young people are supported to think about these principles using structured exercises and discussion. Through this process they get to examine who influences them, who holds power, how to take responsibility for their own actions, how they would like to see their community and what positive change they can effect.

We often use structured exercises to get into conversations about values. For example, one of the exercises we use begins with a brainstorm of the qualities that people look for in friends. Then, through discussion and mutual agreement, we get that list down to half a dozen of the most important qualities. Each young person then has to choose the two qualities they consider most important and buy them using Monopoly money. This always produces some very interesting conversations about friendship, what people are looking for, what they are prepared to give, whether it's possible to find the perfect friend, or whether, in the interest of having some friends, we actually compromise. So, for instance, if an important quality in a friend is someone who never lets you down, does that mean that you don't have many friends because people often do let you down.

The drama group has been working on a play about alcohol. But something that kept coming up again and again was a load of stuff around domestic violence and relationships that the young people in the group have with their fathers in particular, but parents in general. This was coming through implicitly in the sort of scenarios people were creating and acting out which, as it turned out, were actually real live situations for them. So, as workers, we thought it important to recognise what was happening. For one of the workers it was a particularly important issue because she had

cont...

herself come from a position of having a very harrowing relationship with her own father. So it was very important to make this explicit and to create the space to explore these issues in greater depth. So we went on a residential and we said 'OK, we're not doing drama this weekend, this is about domestic violence and our relationships with our families'. The weekend was based on workshops. So for example...(the part-time worker) ran a session on domestic violence. I ran a sort of debate about gender relationships between women and men – what that means for us in terms of our values, our cultural values, our personal values. So there are times when you have to create space to make those kinds of conversations overt. But before that can happen you have to be open to recognising that there is a need.

What's good about the residential setting is that it provides the space and time needed to take your relationship to a different level. It's not like having a two or three hour session and then it's bye-bye at nine o'clock. On a residential, you can carry on. In fact, the conversations that happen at two in the morning are among the most important. But you are also doing things together. Cooking, sharing tasks like washing up. There are spaces that you create which are informal which enable you to see a different side of each other. Crucial within this is the relationship that the workers have with each other. It's very important to communicate well as a team about what's going on, with individuals or the group, and what needs to happen next. But you can only really do that if you feel that you have a shared set of core values and level of commitment with the workers around you.

The weekly sessions help to establish contact and demonstrate a level of commitment. There's this kind of ritual or symbolic negotiation. If I turn up on time, they turn up on time. If they want to talk about something and not do whatever is planned and we respect that, there's another negotiation going on. I think it's a dialogue that we open up with each other as workers and young people. Obviously, if it's a specific project with set outcomes, then it probably has a clear beginning and end. In which case, young people are buying into a product for that particular session. That doesn't mean that we don't have conversations but the session is very much more focused on the outcome and the skills young people are in the process of learning or developing.

(Sangeeta Soni)

Issues

Conversations involve discussion of the whole range of issues important in young people's lives. For example:

Issues about the environment

Through being involved with the youth club, I've been to so many places and done so many things and met so many people that I just wouldn't have. I think my development has been one third me, one third just maturing through the passing of time and one third... (the worker), because I wouldn't have done what I've done and thought about what I've thought about if it wasn't for her. Like when we were younger we used to go to this environmental group and it wasn't that much fun, it was just fun because it was summer and a nice centre and a few nice people there. But eventually, I just never throw litter anymore. Because of that one little group that I went to. I hate throwing litter. It's things like that that you pick up. Also, I know people from all over the world because of the youth exchanges we've been on. And you can just see that slowly but surely things are changing. You don't always realise that when you are younger you just want something to happen now. But things are changing. I've also become much more confident because when I was younger she was the only Asian woman youth worker I knew and I thought that was wonderful because she was like a role model, so I sort of do similar things like not judging people and just giving them a chance.

Issues about health

What I think we're trying to do is to help young people develop the skills to make decisions and choices. So that's what all the information and resources I've developed for youth workers is about, really. It's about saying to them 'Look how are young people going to make choices if they don't have the skills and ability to make those decisions?' Sure, all the resources we've developed have been about health topics but the issue is about the approach. They're not just about information. They're about helping young people to develop the skills to make those decisions. I think that youth workers are particularly well placed to do this work with young people because of the voluntary nature of youth work. Young people come to youth organisations in their own time. They don't have to come. Whereas with parents I think you always aspire for your child to be growing up in a certain way. Schools, although they talk quite a lot about empowering young people, are not really able to do it because the system doesn't allow you to – as much as you might want to. Certainly there may be exceptions because there are some good teachers who are able to do this kind of work, but it's very difficult. So what I come back to is the voluntary relationship and the youth worker's acceptance of that young person as a person because they are used to working with different young people with various backgrounds, various needs, conflicts and problems.

Issues around global inequalities

I would use the accoutrements that young people value as a tool to create change. For example, they value fashion and clothes. So we would look at fashion. I might use a video, for instance, about trainers. How trainers are made. How much the people in Taiwan or wherever they make the trainers get paid a week. How much does it actually cost to make the trainer. And why are they selling you a trainer for £100 when it only costs £20 or £10 or £5 to make? What do you think that's about? In essence, get them to think about this concept that they have about instant gratification. 'How can something that is material make you feel good?' It's a sophisticated argument that you have to keep at a level they understand. Somehow you have to challenge them as to where they are. Young people may resist because in some ways they're quite happy where they are. But, as a youth worker, you know that the impact doesn't necessarily come today or tomorrow. The impact comes six, seven years down the road when you meet a young person who, at one time, was a regular at your unit, and in your interaction with them you can see the growth and development and the measure of the challenges that they had.

Issues around difference and commonality

There's too much going on in the world that's about harming each other. If you look at ethnic cleansing, the wars that go on, the way that young people get treated. All those things. I think if you can make a connection, make someone think about someone else and go beyond their own well-being, then you've done something useful. So that's why I've got a real bee in my bonnet about trying to make connections between people who are different. Particularly culturally or ethnically or racially or religiously different from each other. There's a time bomb out there that will explode sooner or later and actually it's already exploding around us but we are not awake to it. We're nicely, cosily living in our nice little homes with our nice little jobs. We get young people into the youth project but we are creating all of these islands of work with different groups of young people with very little connection between them. What I think we need is more opportunities for young people to find out about each other in terms of the differences that exist between them, for example as Sikh or Muslim, but also be able to explore the common ground between them which may be from the ethics or value base that each of us come from. I think it's about us, as workers, being able to articulate that and being able to enable young people to reflect upon it. So, yes, you can celebrate the differences but you also need to look at what it is we have in common.

'Sensemaking'

However, despite the diversity of contexts and issues, youth workers conversations with young people are essentially about one thing. The development of young people's ability to 'make sense' of themselves and the world. Youth workers' conversations with young people, therefore, provide those much needed opportunities for young people to deliberately and consciously examine their experiences and the meanings they compose for their lives.

But such an exercise is no simple matter since:

*When people talk about their lives, people lie sometimes, forget a lot, exaggerate, become confused and get things wrong. Yet they **are** revealing truths. These truths don't reveal the past 'as it actually was', aspiring to some standard of objectivity. They give us instead the truths of our experiences... Unlike the truth of the scientific ideal, the truths of personal narratives are neither open to proof nor self-evident. We come to understand them only through interpretation, paying careful attention to the contexts that shape their creation and to the world views that inform them.* (Personal Narratives Group quoted in Riessman 1993:22)

People's narratives are, therefore, not 'true' accounts of their experiences but accounts of the 'sense' they have made of their experience. In other words, the interpretations they have woven based on their emotional responses, existing understandings and the social, political and historical contexts within which those understandings and assumptions are located.

However, 'sensemaking' is not a case of constructing reality in the sense of re-interpreting the past to conform to the present, or, alternatively, interpreting the present so as to create a continuous relationship with the past (Berger and Luckman 1967). 'Sensemaking' is a discrete process which has, according to Weick (1995), seven distinct characteristics which distinguish it from other explanatory processes such as understanding and interpretation. For Weick, then, people make sense, that is they come to know what they think, by being able to 'see' what they say. The process of 'sensemaking' is therefore:

1. Grounded in identity construction – since the question of 'who I am' is answered through discovery of how and what I think.

2. Retrospective – in order to learn what I think I look back over what I have said and done in the past.

3. Enactment – by saying and doing things I create new situations which can be inspected for clues about what and how I think; and who I am.

4. Social – what I say, single out (events, actions, thoughts) and conclude are the result of who socialised me, how I was socialised and the 'audience' I anticipate will scrutinise my conclusions.

5. On-going – my talking is spread across time, competes for attention with other on-going projects and is reflected on after it is finished.

6. Focused on and by extracted cues – I single out and embellish a small portion of events, actions and thoughts because I identify them as salient within the context and my personal dispositions.

7. Driven by plausibility rather than accuracy – 'sensemaking' is not about creating accurate accounts but rather accounts which are coherent and credible.

Therefore sensemaking is:

something that preserves plausibility and coherence, something that is reasonable and memorable, something that embodies past experience and expectations, something that resonates with other people, something that can be constructed retrospectively but also can be used prospectively, something that captures both feelings and thought, something that allows for embellishment to fit current oddities, something that is fun to construct. In short, what is necessary in sensemaking is a good story. (Weick 1995:60)

However, 'personal stories are not merely a way of telling someone (or oneself) about one's life; they are the means by which identities may be fashioned.' (Rosenwald and Ochberg quoted in Riessman 1993:2) Therefore, a person's identity is to be found in their capacity to 'keep a particular narrative going' (Giddens 1991:54) since:

Self-identity [in other words] is not something that is just given, as a result of the continuities of the individual's action-system, but something that has to be routinely created and sustained in the reflexive activities of the individual. (Giddens 1991:52)

'Sensemaking' is, therefore, a process of self actualisation, the moral thread of which is authenticity, that is being true to oneself – a process that requires being able to find oneself as well as being able to disentangle the true self from the false self. (Giddens 1991:79)

The role of the youth worker, as I have said earlier, is therefore to engage with young people in the process of moral philosophising which:

- enables them to develop a consistent set of values
- informs their identity
- supports their development of virtue as authentic human beings

In the process, workers need to remember that 'sensemaking' is an integrated activity. People do not usually stop to make sense, they do it as they are going along, (Wallemacq and Sims 1998) reflecting critically on their experience and creating new meanings for their lives.

Part three
The art of youth work

The 'art of youth work' is the ability to make and sustain meaningful relationships with young people within which they engage in the process of moral philosophising. A process which enables and supports young people to develop their sense of identity and cultivate themselves as authentic human beings.

This is achieved through voluntary relationships with young people established within a framework of acceptance and valuing young people, honesty, trust, respect and reciprocity. Through the use of reflective 'dialogue', youth workers support young people to learn from their experience and make sense of themselves, their lives and their world.

In order to successfully undertake such work, youth workers need to be skilled, not only in the areas of groupwork and facilitating learning from experience, but also in the more equivocal areas of effective communication, honesty, friendliness, humour, patience and boundary setting.

Central to this are youth workers' values, since values underpin youth work, impact on it and form the basis for young people's moral reflections and exploration. In order to become effective practitioners, youth workers therefore need to commit themselves to continuous reflective practice so as to constantly revisit, review and renew their values and underlying ethical framework.

However, in an occupation like youth work, reflection and discussions about principles and values are not merely intellectual exercises since there is an intention that 'discussion' should lead to both individual and collective action through 'the **activity** of talking and the chain of conversations in which the individual takes part...as well as its **content** (Hardy, Lawrence and Phillips 1998).

Therefore, understanding participation, for example, involves not only an intellectual understanding but also acting in ways which enable young people to participate which, in turn, requires an understanding of the concept of participation. The process is somewhat circular but represents what Plato called 'philosophy' (an understanding of virtue) and 'habit' (a disposition towards acting virtuously) which he considered to be the two essential components of an ethical education. (Kupperman 1983)

The training and development of youth workers, therefore, needs to include, at its very core, an ethical education which seeks to extend workers' personal and professional philosophy; and encourage their 'intelligent disposition' towards acting virtuously – a disposition which requires the exercise of practical reason and judgement within a 'coherent system of precepts' or ethical framework.

Such an approach is crucial, not only because of the opportunity it offers for personal development, but also because youth workers need to be, themselves, well versed in the process of moral philosophising through which they seek to support young people.

Skills and values

Youth workers need highly developed and effective interpersonal skills in order to establish and build positive relationships with young people. They also need groupwork facilitation skills and an understanding of group dynamics; an ability to critically appraise and evaluate practice; an understanding of how she or he uses him or herself in practice; a knowledge of the context within which one is working – social, political, economic, and an ability to act as an advocate when necessary, but also knowing when to enable young people to speak for themselves.

Youth workers need to be confident and comfortable about their own identity and how that has shaped their own values and beliefs. He or she needs to be able to be articulate and express what these are.

Youth workers need to be able to engage with other professionals from different fields and with parents. We need to see young people as a part of their community and work so that the community sees them as stakeholders in it.

We also need not to be 'experts'. It can be very reassuring to a young person to hear an adult say 'I don't know' or 'I never thought of that' or 'I don't understand' as often young people are afraid to say these things. They see it as a sign of weakness. We also need to know our own limitations and be able to say 'I'm sorry' or 'I was wrong' or 'I shouldn't have done that'. We need to be accountable to young people for our actions as well as to those who mange and fund us.

cont...

This might seem obvious but youth workers need to like young people. Need to get a kick out of working with them. Need to enjoy their energy, laughter, spontaneity and tendency to be politically incorrect. It can be very refreshing.

(Teresa Geraghty)

Youth work offers young people opportunities to engage in the process of 'moral inquiry' through which they are enabled and supported to:

- explore their values
- reflect on the principles of their own moral judgements
- make reasoned choices that can be sustained through committed action

Through this reflective process, young people gain and develop the capacities to:

- learn from their experience
- engage in critical and reflective thinking
- 'make sense' of themselves and their world

In order to successfully undertake this work, youth workers need particular skills – including those identified above – interpersonal and groupwork skills, an ability to advocate with and for young people, a knowledge of the context of his/her work, an understanding of how she or he uses him or herself in practice and an ability to critically appraise and evaluate practice.

Effective youth workers must also earn the trust and respect of young people and the communities in which they work.

There is that trust from your parents' side as well. Say, for instance it I got caught in trouble with the police or I met someone and I wanted to be with her and maybe get married to her. Now the thing is I couldn't approach my parents with that. I would come and speak to...(the worker) and ask him to have a word with my father. I would ask him to explain the situation and provide me with support.

There is partly an assumption of trust in the community – trusting the worker to be non-judgmental – unconditional positive regard for them as human beings.

Last year I wanted to go to Pakistan with the youth project and I told my parents about it and they just smiled at me and said 'OK, son, you're going to Pakistan'. But the more into it I got then my parents said 'Oh you can't go because who is going to take care of you?' and things like that. I spoke to...(the worker) and he spoke to my parents and, because he spoke to them about the project and they knew he was older and wiser and he'd been there before, they gave me the chance to go with him because they gave him that responsibility to take care of me.

Skills

But what other skills do youth workers need to undertake effective youth work?

Youth workers need good communication skills. They need the skills to understand how to relate to young people on their level. Skills to listen and empathise. They need to have the skills that enable them to have a positive relationship with young people – a friendly character (but not a friend), be humorous (but not the joker), they need to set boundaries (but not appear to be authoritarian).

In order to be a good youth worker you have to have commitment. You have to be honest. You have to believe that you can make a difference. Have some faith in yourself and also in the people around you. Sometimes you'll see a gem in a young person and you think there is some potential or talent there. So it's about being able to recognise that talent or potential and developing ways of making that gem become a jewel in some way that is wonderfully polished. That means being able to make connections on behalf of young people and seeking out and seizing opportunities for them to further their interests and talents.

Youth workers have to be empathetic. You have to care about young people. You also have to be very observant and aware of what is happening within individuals and the group and the part that we are all playing in different situations.

My work with young people with learning disabilities means that you have to be very patient. You have to give a lot more time to young people to give them the opportunity to really listen and to speak in their own way and in their own language. For example, sometimes we have young people with speech difficulties who we find quite difficult to understand. In those situations, it's really important that we don't pretend we have understood if we haven't. We know we haven't heard and so do they. They know we're bluffing. So it's really important to give that time, however embarrassed or guilty you may feel, because what's important is that the young person gets to express himself or herself. Some young people can write or draw, so for them we may get some paper. We also do some signing with the young people who know how. For the young people who can't speak, we watch body language. And, because we take a long time building a relationship with that young person, we gradually get to understand what different movements mean. By all kinds of methods we actually do get to know what each young person is telling us.

To me, the most important skill of the youth worker is the skill of supporting young people to complete their learning cycle. Young people have a lot of experiences but, from a developmental point of view, the most important thing is the understanding and learning that they gain from those experiences. So, instead of simply having an experience or reacting to a situation, young people are encouraged to reflect on it, consider alternatives and then decide what they will take away from that experience in terms of what they think or do. That process may involve role-play or other activities that explore human attitudes and behaviour. The main thing is to help young people to become aware of the process. I'm not in favour of young people not knowing what's happening to them.

So youth workers need to have good communication skills and the ability to listen and empathise. They need to be honest, friendly, humorous, observant, patient and be able to set boundaries. They need to have commitment, faith in themselves and those around them and be able to support young people through their learning cycle.

However, such skills are not practised in a vacuum. Youth work is underpinned by youth workers' understanding of young people's lives.

Young people are the experts of their own world. Our responsibility is not to know it, but to try to understand a little of it – just as much as they want to offer. That certainly helps me to be mindful about how I work with them so that I'm not going to offend them unknowingly or make them feel uncomfortable or open a door and quickly close it again. Then it's about creating the situations for them to want to take the plunge, if you like – to make some choices. And then being there to support and help them think about what they learned, or how they could have dealt with the situation in a different way, or how they could have made it more beneficial or successful – without causing them to feel like they're rubbish or made a big mistake.

Young people often say that adults don't understand. That we've forgotten. I think that's often true. Sure, we can talk about the characteristic of adolescence but we don't always remember what it actually felt like and the impact those changes have on you as a young person. So I think the job is about listening and hearing. It's about seeing things with a 16-year-old pair of eyes, not using the hindsight that I have at thirty something and saying, well you know this will happen. It's actually about trying to understand how they see it, how big it is to them and what's important about it to them. Not what's important to us. OK, it might not be big in two weeks time but in that moment it is big and needs to be afforded the same significance we attach to the things we identify as important. The main thing is to affirm young people and their experience – what they are saying and what they are feeling. After all, who feels it knows it.

The relationship and work is, also, sometimes enhanced by some particular characteristic of the worker:

For some people it helps that…(the worker) is a Muslim. They would feel more comfortable talking to him knowing that he is a Muslim as well. I feel more comfortable talking to him because we are both Pakistani. It's just one of those things really. It just helps you to build up trust knowing that he's from the same religion.

I'm not an overtly religious person. I fast and attend Friday prayer but I wouldn't call myself a religious person because you're meant to pray five times a day and that's what I class as religious. The fact that...(the worker) is a Muslim is completely irrelevant to me. The only time it has helped me is when we've had a talk on religion and he has been there and been able to answer my questions. But that's because he just happened to be there and he's more educated than I am. The thing is, though, that...(the worker) can speak Punjabi and the first time he came up to me and spoke to me in Punjabi, I was really taken aback. Then he asked me what village I was from. And I thought 'how do you know these things?'. It broke down some barriers and kind of made the whole relationship relaxed and more personal. The Punjabi language is my identity. Most of my friends can't speak Punjabi, they speak a different dialect. So...(the worker) speaking Punjabi makes me feel closer to him because he knows where I was from.

If...(the worker) was a white worker I think there'd be a lot more mistrust. I don't know why. But I do think it would probably take more time to actually trust him because you'd have to work much harder on the relationship and you'd be thinking in your head all the time 'Is he thinking I'm a bad person because I talk like this'. In your head you'd probably be picking out the little things and feeling uneasy and wondering if he understands the culture. Does he understand what goes on at home? And thinking, he can't really. Unless you've lived it you can't really know what's going on.

However, the bottom line is not necessarily a worker's array of skills (although skills are important) and neither is it about their particular characteristics (although this is also important). The bottom line of good youth work practice rests on the worker's values.

It's about attitude. Accepting where young people are coming from. Not putting them down but gaining their trust and being able to explore with them. There's a difference between a young person saying something and you just telling them they shouldn't have said it; and letting them say it and working out what's the belief underneath it. It's about adults who accept and value young people and who don't see themselves as somehow above them. That's where you have to be to start as a youth worker. Then the most important skill you need is listening. The other important skill is gaining young people's interest. So much so that they want to know

cont...

more. That, I think, comes from getting to know them over a long period of time. It comes from creating the right atmosphere for them to be able to ask about anything.

Being non-judgmental is very important. So, if my values are different from a young woman's parents' values, then I need to explain to her what I believe without judging her parents as wrong, because in the end she has to choose. You can't be in the position of turning her against her family. She has to grow into someone different if she chooses. The role of the worker is to open up the possibility that there is another point of view.

A youth worker is another adult who is not a parent or a teacher. Because Guiders are volunteers, lots of them have another job, so the girls get an insight into another profession which they might never have got. It's different to being a relation because you are completely outside of everything else the young woman does. You are not part of her school or her family and she's probably known you for quite a long time, coming through the Brownies and Guides, and, later, the Rangers. So there is continuity. Having a range of women of different generations also creates a wonderful tapestry of different perspectives – what different people have done with their lives, their different experiences, the different skills they have to share.

(Jennie Lamb)

Values

A youth worker's values are important not only because they impact directly on the work...

As a youth worker you can't impinge your own values on young people. I come from a background that is very middle class and work with young people that are at the lower socio-economic class in terms of their parents being unemployed and things like that. It would be very easy for me to say 'Well you should be doing this or you should be doing that'. So I think youth workers need to make sure that they look at their own values. And particularly in terms of how their values affect the way they are working with young people and dealing with the particular issues they are working with.

The youth worker needs to be constantly aware of her or his own prejudices and bias when it comes to combating structural inequalities. In terms of Northern Ireland, you have to be aware that very few venues are perceived as 'neutral', and often young people do not feel safe travelling outside of their own areas. Even a simple thing like wearing a particular football shirt can be divisive, provocative and dangerous. Words and phrases can also be insulting and derogatory without the young person knowing this to the full extent. There is also a lot of distrust and a lack of knowledge about the facts of history. In Northern Ireland there are always two versions of every story and very few workers who know both – including me!

...but because the worker's values both underpin the work and form the basis for young people's moral reflections and exploration.

My values are central to the way I work with young people. I feel quite privileged coming from a spiritual base, which is a Hindu base, because I don't feel any need to evangelise. But there are things about my values which come from my spirituality that I think are also common to people in general – like not wanting to hurt other people, taking on board that your actions may have an impact on other people, so you have to think about what it is you are doing. You could even go back to the Ten Commandments, I suppose, if you wanted to say don't kill, don't steal and the basic differentiation between good and evil that is there in everybody's faith. Issues around honesty, for example. Doing unto others as you wish to be treated yourself, which is one of those core themes that I think is universal but we don't talk about anymore. I think another important value is about taking the time to reflect on your life. Wanting to give other people a chance is another. All of these are part and parcel of the values I hold and consider crucial in my relationships with young people.

Being non-judgmental and accepting young people as they are is the key. Everybody has strengths and weaknesses. You can work with those, and, through working with the strengths, you can help develop their weaknesses. Some young people have a great deal of knowledge about issues but they haven't got the skills or the information to actually deal with those issues in their ordinary everyday lives. So you would hope that, if and when you come to work with them around, say, particular health issues, whether it's smoking or whatever, they would come to see the issues around the topic and, hopefully, give up smoking. And that's not about trying to drive them into any particular box. It's not about saying you must not do this or you must do that. It's about giving them the options in the hope that they will then, with skills and knowledge, make decisions that will help them in the future.

My search for understanding is a part of my faith. It gives me something to fall back on. It means I don't have to have all the answers. What I do have is a way of working through my questions, and an ethical framework that helps me to make sense of the issues around me. As a youth worker, my faith helps me to support young people to find a path that's clear for them. I help them to make sense of the spiritual teachings they have received, and consider how to relate these to their everyday life – particularly when they need to come through a difficult time.

My values affect my relationships with young people through them realising that I don't mean them any harm, I do have their interest at heart and that my contact with them is borne out of honesty, respect, caring – all of which come from a deeper commitment to people in general, but to them in particular, because that's the area I'm working in. I think if they know that, and most of them do, then the relationship can operate at a greater depth. So that would mean that they would be able to openly ask questions about doubts they might have about their lives. There may be experiences in their lives that are pivotal and may be harmful or hurtful to them, that perhaps they can share with me in confidence. Actually, many of the young people I work with do come with some very damaging things that have happened to them. They feel able to talk about these because they sense that the relationship with me operates at a different level from the relationships they may have with other adults.

Ethical issues, problems and dilemmas

In the process, youth workers encounter a range of ethical issues, problems and dilemmas. Some of these may arise because they are 'working' [which involves specific duties and responsibilities] with 'young people' [who may have fewer rights and may be regarded as vulnerable in some way] (Banks 1997). Others may concern issues of confidentiality or dilemmas about the need to safeguard the welfare of different individuals and groups – e.g. the young person, the community, the agency. (Morgan and Banks 1999)

Whatever the specifics of the situation, ethical issues emerge as a result of conflicting values – between the worker and employing agency, parents, the local community, colleagues or allied agencies. Sometimes it is an internal conflict between the worker and his or her own conscience. It goes almost without saying that these are never easy to resolve. But, despite the existence of both principles for practice (e.g. Biestek, 1961, cited in Banks, 1995) and models of ethical decision making (see Banks 1997), there still remains a question about the underlying values and ethical framework which inform workers' interpretations and decisions about ethical concerns and their own future action.

As a youth worker, working with young people with disabilities, it's very difficult to know where the balance is between what is practical and what, in an ideal world, should actually be happening. I sometimes face terrible dilemmas of wondering how much I should be talking with young people about contraceptives or relationships, for example. Not just about the physical aspects, but in terms of the feelings and what relationships actually mean to them. I ask myself 'When do they have the space to do that?' And the truth is, they often don't. There is so much anxiety and pressure from parents, guardians who have an influential role and others, that there's never any time or space or privacy for them to discover what relationships mean to them. So, whilst I might want to support young people to think about those things, I know some parents would not find that acceptable.

It is very difficult to work with young people in Northern Ireland around the issue of identity. And, while political education and cross-community work has been on the youth service curriculum since 1987, I think it's very difficult to be effective if nothing happens with adults in the community while young people are engaged in their programme. But it's not only that young people are seen to be divorced from their community, it's also that so many parents are actually openly opposed to cross community work.

Reflective practice

Certainly, workers need to be:

conscious of their own values and priorities in the work...aware of how these differ from, and conflict with, those of others and...prepared, either to justify and defend their views, or to change or modify them. (Banks 1997:25)

However, what is needed is more than this. For youth workers also need, as a matter of routine, to constantly revisit, reflect on and renew their values. Such a commitment to reflective practice requires practitioners to:

- Question 'taken-for-granted' assumptions about the definition of problems and categorisation of need.
- Recognise the ways in which ideas, thoughts, understandings and opinions are shaped historically, economically, politically and socially through social structures and processes.
- Make the implicit explicit.
- Raise the profile of value positions and working with the problematics they generate
- Locate practice in its agency contexts, so that service delivery issues are not addressed as routine constraints.
- Build reflection, involvement and evaluation into every stage of the practice process. (Everitt, Hardiker, Littlewood and Mullender 1992:134)

A commitment to reflecting on your own practice is crucial. You need to be able to acknowledge your mistakes and accept criticism. So, if a young person says 'You were wrong to do that to me', then you have to take it on board and come clean.

Youth workers have to be open to their own learning. They need a commitment to training and a commitment to looking at their own practice, and really reflecting on the way they work with young people. That's really important to me. It matters because it's people's lives you're working with and so getting it right or being on the right track to working positively with them is very important. I learn so much from them as well, and I love that.

In the end, however, the need for youth workers' clarity and commitment in relation to their values is not simply because of the necessity to develop critical reflective practice or resolve ethical dilemmas. The need arises from the necessity for youth workers to be, themselves, well versed in the reflective and deliberative processes through which they seek to support young people.

Indeed, the idea that those involved in social education should engage in philosophical reflection is not new. Pring (1984) suggested that a part of the 'professional job of those who introduce personal and social education into the curriculum' should include:

> *A careful, philosophical reflection upon what it means to be a person, how development as a person is inextricably linked with a form of social life, and where moral values and ideas are presupposed in both.* (Pring 1984:167).

Earlier, Davies and Gibson had emphasised the need for the worker to 'understand what sort of person he himself is, what his needs are and what his beliefs and values are.' (1967:186)

And earlier still, the McNair Committee had commented that:

> *A well-informed philosophy of life, which may or may not be professedly religious, is most necessary to the youth leader; indeed, it is not easy to conceive of a successful youth leader without it.* (HMSO 1944:101)

But these are not simply old concerns. As recently as 1999, the report of the 1996–99 Youth Work Development Grants Programme identified 'peak performing' youth workers as having personal qualities rooted in:

- a clear set of values
- professional integrity
- a constant openness to self-appraisal and learning (Hunter, Payne, Pittham and Young 1999:7)

So, 'philosophy' is not enough since a 'well-informed philosophy of life' can only have (professional) integrity if it informs action. That is to say, it is not enough to know what is 'right', one must also seek to act 'rightly'.

The challenge for youth work, then, is how to support workers to develop their 'philosophy' in terms of a clear set of values; and their 'integrity' in terms of a disposition towards acting ethically – that is, a disposition towards finding right action in particular circumstances and acting from right motive.

Philosophy and the habit

> *The problem is that most people only have the vaguest idea of what it might be to lead an ethical life. They understand ethics as a system of rules forbidding us to do things. They do not grasp it as a basis for thinking about how we are to live. They live largely self-interested lives, not because they are born selfish, but because the alternatives seem awkward, embarrassing, or just plain pointless. They cannot see any way of making an impact on the world, and, if they could, why should they bother? Short of undergoing a religious conversion, they see nothing to live for except the pursuit of their own material self-interest. But the possibility of living an ethical life provides us with a way out of this impasse.* (Singer 1997: vi)

For the youth worker, it is not so much a question of leading an ethical life, but developing an ethical practice – assuming, indeed, that such things can be so easily separated. Nonetheless, the emphasis here is on the development of the practitioner as an agent engaged in the kind of youth work practice described in earlier chapters of this book. That is, a 'youth work' which seeks to:

- Support young people's moral deliberations and learning – about what is 'good' and conducive to the good life generally.

- Help young people to develop the skill of rational judgement – enabling them to make reasoned choices and decisions which can be sustained through committed action.

- Encourage the development of virtue – in the sense that young people would choose to act in certain ways based on a 'disposition' towards certain ideals. (Williams 1993:9)

Ethics

This approach to ethics is different from:

- a code of ethics – which is concerned with standard setting and regulation, in the sense that it offers a 'code' or guide to 'professional' conduct, and stipulates the nature and exercise of sanctions; or

- considerations of the ethical issues and dilemmas which workers encounter – for example, in relation to confidentiality, autonomy and control, agency policy, individual and public welfare, accountability to funders, and so on.

However, while both of these approaches make their own particular contribution to the development of practice, they are based on a premise that workers have (enough of) an understanding of the values involved to enable them to interpret an ethical code and resolve ethical dilemmas. This, of course, is not necessarily so.

For it is one thing to declare that the values underlying youth and community work are respect for:

- basic human rights – e.g. justice, freedom
- the individual and rights to self-determination
- the different cultures and religions in society (NYA 1997c)

It is quite another matter to interpret or implement such principles in the absence of a clear understanding of the concept of 'respect' – never mind justice or freedom.

Yet, it is possible to go further. One could offer illustrations of what 'respect' might mean – for example, as do Crimmens and Whalen (1999) when they comment that 'respect for human rights' includes 'listening to young people, taking their views seriously, giving them information and involving them in decision making about their lives'. This is helpful, but, as Robin Barrow points out:

> There is a distinction between stating clearly 'what I mean by democracy is one man, one vote' in order to advance a discussion in a history lesson about whether Periclean Athens was or was not democratic, and attempting to analyse the concept of democracy which would involve one in a more painstaking task which would have nothing specifically to do with Athens. (Barrow 1981:135)

It is not such a straightforward matter, then, of being guided by a code of 'professional ethics', or having the capacity to recognise the ethical problems and dilemmas involved in the work. For, central to these activities, is the ability to interpret the meaning of the concepts and values involved. In youth work, this includes concepts such as education, participation, empowerment and equality of opportunity; and values such as justice and freedom.

> In terms of their training, youth workers need a clear understanding of their role and the fact that youth work is a job. They need to reflect on practice, and they need to learn how to set boundaries and hold them. There are also some skills like groupwork, facilitation skills and dealing with conflict, which are important. But something that is, in some ways, more important is the opportunity to engage in a positive personal development experience. The sort of experience that encourages you to explore your views, hopes, fears, aspirations, values, what being you means to you and how your experiences have shaped your values and your life. Really, it's about the development of them as people. It's almost like going through the same sort of experience they will be engaging in with young people. In 'Starting From Strengths', there was a recognition that, in the first six months, part-time staff were often having a personal development experience themselves, rather than working with the young people. That was right in the sense that they needed the time and attention to reflect and develop as practitioners.

But sometimes, when people leave college courses, they haven't themselves had that sort of experience. If they are going to help young people to understand themselves and their lives, then I really do think that they need to have experienced it themselves.

But how are youth workers to be encouraged and supported to explore their 'views, hopes, fears, aspirations, values, experiences' in relation, not only to themselves as people, but in terms of their role as youth workers?

[For] surely it was Dewey who, in modern times, foresaw that education had to be redefined as the fostering of thinking, rather than the transmission of knowledge; that there could be no difference in the method by which teachers were taught and the methods by which they would be expected to teach; that the logic of a discipline must not be confused with the sequence of discoveries that would constitute its understanding; that student reflection is best stimulated by living experience, rather than by formally organised, dessicated text; that reasoning is sharpened and perfected by disciplined discussion as by nothing else, and that reasoning skills are essential for successful reading and writing; and that the alternative to indoctrinating students with values is to help them to reflect effectively on the values that are constantly being urged on them. (Lipman 1988 quoted in Whalley 1991:69)

Lipman's reference to teachers is no less relevant to youth workers, in the sense that there should be no difference in the method by which youth workers are trained, and the methods by which they are expected to work with young people. So youth workers need to be able to think. Their reflection is best stimulated by living experience. Their reasoning should be sharpened and perfected by disciplined discussion. And they should be helped to reflect effectively on the values that are constantly being urged on them, and those which the practice of youth work demands.

Such 'disciplined discussion', within the context of reflecting on values, could be envisaged as containing three components.

1. Serious discussion about values, including getting people to see what it is like to live according to various value judgements (including the destructive effect of immorality on psychological harmony and integrity).
2. Promotion of sensitivity to others and the consequences of one's actions.
3. Discussion of moral rules and principles – e.g. respect for persons.
   (Kupperman 1983)

Such discussion should, following Dewey, focus on workers' own personal and work experiences, and help them to reflect effectively on the values which inform and underpin their lives and their work as youth workers.

Clearly, then, the process is not value-free. The idea is not to produce 'rational egoists', but to support a 'rational form of morality, which enables a person to adopt a stance that is critical of tradition but not subjective' (Peters 1981:143).

For Peters, this cannot be achieved purely through one's ability to reason 'in the sense of making inferences'. Rational morality must be characterised by the ability to reason:

- supported by a group of 'rational passions connected with the demands of consistency, order, clarity and relevance'; and
- [what Piaget calls] 'reversibility in thought'. In other words, the person must be able to appreciate the experiences of others and show concern for their interests as well as one's own. They must be able to demonstrate what David Hume called a 'sentiment for humanity' or, in other words, empathy. (Peters 1981:144)

'Philosophy' or the nature of virtue

According to Socrates, a person cannot be truly virtuous unless they knew what virtue is. The only way to obtain such knowledge, he believed, was to examine accounts of the particular virtues and seek to expose their 'nature'. (Gottlieb 1997)

We therefore find, in Plato's *Laches*, an exchange in which Socrates dismisses all the examples of courage being offered by Laches by insisting 'What is the common quality that is called courage, and which includes all of the various uses of the term when applied both to pleasure and pain, and in all the cases to which I was just now referring?' (Plato 1970:117)

In *Lysis*, Socrates cajoles Lysis and Menexenus into a debate about 'the nature of friendship' (Plato 170:91). Temperance gets the same treatment in *Charmides* when Socrates tells Charmides to:

fix your attention more closely and look within you; consider the effect which temperance has upon yourself, and the nature of that which should have this effect. Think over all this, and tell me truly and courageously – What is temperance? (Plato 1970:47)

And, in *The Republic*, while debating justice and injustice, Glaucon says 'I want to be told what exactly each of them is and what effects it has as such on the mind of its possessor, leaving aside any question of rewards or consequences'. (Plato 1974:103)

Form and Content

However, while many of Socrates' investigations end with no final conclusions, the dialogues themselves act as the vehicle for expounding the many and various thoughts about, perceptions and interpretations of the topics being discussed. So, following Kupperman's (1983) form of 'serious discussion about values' and 'discussion of moral rules and principles', it is possible to envisage a content which supports workers to explore the 'nature' of justice or freedom or empowerment. A 'dialogue' which draws on their own experiences to give meaning to their conception of such principles and values.

In addition, while it may seem erroneous that Plato's dialogues often involve Socrates' intellectual adversaries agreeing with him about the nature of justice or courage or friendship, it is equally unrealistic to operate on the basis that people can believe anything they like – i.e. that there are no guiding principles for life and that one opinion is as valid as the next. For example, that a racist or sexist perspective is as valid as any other because it is someone's opinion. There is no suggestion here that we should be so liberal. After all, Socrates did not question the 'worthiness' of courage. He sought to reveal the nature of courage (justice, friendship, etc.) because he believed that knowledge of virtue was the same as being virtuous. In other words, that to know the **nature** of courage was the same as being courageous because, so Socrates believed, no-one having such knowledge would choose to behave otherwise. His search for definition was, therefore, a means to an end – namely the exercise of virtue. (Gottlieb 1997) A conviction shared by Aristotle:

> the object of our enquiry is not to know the nature of virtue but become ourselves virtuous…it is necessary, therefore, to consider the right way of performing actions, for it is actions, as we have said, that determine the character of the resulting moral states. (Aristotle 1987:44)

For Aristotle, then, a person acquires virtue by doing virtuous acts. 'It is by doing just acts that we become just, by doing temperate acts that we become temperate, by doing courageous acts that we become courageous.' (Aristotle 1987:43)

Of course, 'disciplined discussion' within youth work may seek to question the 'worthiness' of justice or empowerment or equality of opportunity. But what must also be central to such deliberations is the illumination or 'revelation' of their **nature**. And particularly, an understanding of their nature in terms of what action one would take in becoming just or empowering or promoting equality.

'Habit' or the practice of virtue

The contention here, then, is that 'philosophical reflection' does not lead to 'a well-informed philosophy of life' unless it contains both an understanding of the nature of virtue and the practice of virtue. And that, therefore, any 'personal development experience' for youth workers must necessarily include, not only discussion about the meaning or nature of various principles, values and virtues, but also an exploration of the ways in which they, as workers, are themselves virtuous. That is, the ways in which they demonstrate virtue through their own actions and practice.

Notwithstanding, actions performed in accordance with virtue are not performed because the actions are **themselves** virtuous – e.g. just or trustworthy or respectful. Actions performed in accordance with virtue require that the person performing them satisfy three conditions:

1. The person should know what they are doing.

2. They should deliberately choose to do it for its own sake.

3. They should do it as an instance of a settled moral state. (Aristotle 1987:50)

This is because, for Aristotle, virtue is not simply a habit but an:

> internalised disposition of action, desire and feeling. It is an intelligent disposition. It involves the agent's exercise of judgement, that same quality of practical reason. (Williams 1993:35)

Virtue, therefore, requires not only habit but 'an intelligent disposition' involving practical reason and judgement. However, although one makes judgements and exercises the capacity for critical thinking, choice is not simply a matter of reason. For:

> as Plato and Aristotle remind us, behind the choice of actions lies the choice of dispositions, of characters, of overall patterns of life...dispositions cannot be switched on and off in deference to the calculation of likely consequences on particular occasions...the practical choice will be between one fairly persistent disposition and others, equally persistent, that contrast with it. And if we then ask what sort of person it is in one's own interest to be, what dispositions it is advantageous to have, there is little doubt that it will be ones that can be seen as virtues...as dispositions that harmonise with knowledge, but also, more specifically, in the light of some conception of the good, and with some respect for the way of life of the society in which one lives. (Mackie 1990:192)

Culture and structure

The concern is about dominant cultures and where people come from into youth work as part-time workers. So the dominant culture for a police officer would be the culture that he or she is employed in. If that person then wanted to go into youth work, they bring with them those dominant cultural values. It's the same for people who work in hierarchical situations in factories or shops where there is a clearly defined hierarchy, function and purpose; it's about profit, and all of those things are actually dominant cultural

cont...

influences. They then step into the youth service and we expect them to be something else. And we expect them to be something else almost by inclination. That they are going to be able to forget those dominant cultural values and accept the culture that is dominant within youth service, or the culture that we perhaps wish would be dominant, because very often it isn't. And so the challenge for training is about getting the part-time worker, the deliverer of the service, to understand and internalise the value base of youth work. Actually, that's the crucial bit, but we miss it because we are scared about money and whether or not we have it. So training ends up being related to functions. You know – how do you organise this trip to ice-skating, or manage the centre, or look after the bureaucracy of what's going on. And so we do not get the part-time worker to explore the issues of values and dominant cultures, because it's considered to be too nebulous and esoteric. There is also a false belief by many training managers that, if they get people into the training arena, they're only going to get them once and so they need to teach them the things that are important. How to fill in their time sheets, health and safety, what to do in terms of child abuse. All very important issues but still not preparing people to do youth work with young people – in this almost nonsensical view that we have about what the culture of youth work is.

The other thing is, you do not train part-time teachers. You do not train part-time nurses. What you train are nurses or teachers who work part-time. And that is exactly the philosophy that underpins youth work training in Wales. That actually means that the structure of youth work training in Wales, from the time that people take their first step into it, they are actually training to become full-time youth workers. What they actually do is make decisions within that training about when they are going to get off, or whether they are going to continue. So there is a vision in Wales that part-time workers, particularly key part-time workers, will be trained to at least Certificate (in Higher Education) level. And that's actually where part-time workers are now starting to get off this continuous and coherent training route we have here in Wales. This involves 21 of the 22 authorities, and some voluntary organisations. But, because the voluntary sector, through the Council for Wales Voluntary Youth Services (CWVYS), also has it's own initial training course, it becomes crucial to build a bridge between voluntary and maintained sector training. And what we are doing is running

cont...

an introductory course that focuses on what the youth service is, what it does, what it is built on and what it is driven by. Thereby integrating both voluntary and maintained sectors at a strategic level.

(John Rose)

The approach to training outlined here would necessarily require a change in both the culture and structure of current youth work training. And this is particularly so, given the prominence accorded to a 'personal development programme' involving the investigation of particular principles, values and virtues; and attention to the development of virtue in workers.

This, as envisaged, would form the centre-piece of youth work training with the theoretical underpinnings (e.g. psychology, sociology, social policy) and practical skills (e.g. groupwork) acting to both inform and enrich this essentially philosophical exercise.

In terms of culture, this would involve:

- Students/workers taking responsibility for their learning.
- An integrated approach to the training of full-time and part-time workers.
- An organisational commitment to the continuous development of both full-time and part-time workers through a structured supervision process based on learning from experience and providing opportunities for workers to:
  - develop their skills in critical thinking
  - engage in disciplined discussion about values and moral principles
  - develop the practice of virtue through action, reflection and learning.

In terms of structure, this may involve:

- teaching or tutoring – for the acquisition of knowledge
- coaching – for the acquisition of skills
- mentoring – for the acquisition of insight, understanding and wisdom (Clutterbuck and Sweeney 1997:3)

Indeed, the idea that youth workers could benefit from coaching and mentoring during their training was advocated in *Starting From Strengths* (Bolger and Scott 1984), and further developed in the *Handbook for Personal Training Advisers* (Jackson, Bolger and Young 1989), which described the personal training adviser as offering advice and guidance; and facilitating learning from experience through an open, trusting and personal developmental relationship with the trainee. This was an approach developed specifically in relation to the training of part-time youth and community workers. An approach which may, nonetheless, be equally as beneficial in the continuous support and development of both full-time and part-time workers.

> *Initial training is not enough. Youth workers' personal and professional development is inter-linked. Some youth workers, especially those based in centres, are very de-motivated, mainly because they are not using their professional skills and talents, and are really glorified administrators and caretakers. There is a need for some kind of professional organisation in Northern Ireland that could stimulate debate and discussion on youth work practice so that workers wouldn't feel so isolated. Some workers do not receive any supervision and those in the voluntary sector may have to develop their management committee as well as the young people.*

> *One of the problems for a lot of youth workers is they work on their own. Although they work with other people, it's actually quite isolating. There is a distance between them and the young people. There is a distance between them and the part-time staff that they have managerial responsibility for. They may be on a venue like a school where their professionalism isn't recognised or is seen as different. So they can be isolated and, as a consequence, it's actually easy to get diverted or lose focus. So I think one of the roles of management is to help them regain that focus and to put their experiences in perspective. It's also about helping them to see some of the positives of their work and their achievements when they can often feel like they are not getting anywhere. Sometimes it's also about helping them where they are blocked in their learning cycle. But consistently it's about keeping them focused on the fundamental question that we also ask young people. 'Do you think it's the right thing to do?' Because, whatever decision they make, they are the ones who have to live with it.*

> *Youth workers need a range of practice opportunities in working with individuals and groups. They also need, and I think this is very important, time to reflect on their practice and themselves as practitioners. Actually, that's one area where I think part-time workers should be given much more support and encouragement – time for reflection.*

My work is very much about the personal empowerment of young people. The personal right of actually being able to say 'no' to somebody. It's very encouraging when you see a young person doing that or when you see a young person who would normally run to the workers to resolve every minor conflict actually taking on some incident and dealing with it themselves. But this needs to be geared at the right level. Providing the support and working with the young person to discover what is acceptable to them in terms of what they can take on. It has to be geared at the right

cont...

level and the right pace, and supported by the right actions. And when I use the word right, I mean in terms of what is helpful for the development of that particular individual.

Those who support or supervise part-time workers have a responsibility to value them, listen to them, support their efforts, their risk taking and innovations. Encourage them to reflect. Really model the youth work process that you would expect from them in relation to their work with young people. The service's commitment to valuing people, honesty, trust, respect, should be at all levels of the service. It's not just something we save for young people. It should be there for everyone.

The best support would be someone who has similar values. Although there is the danger, of course, that you might just end up supporting each other's bad habits or bad values. So, again, it's about a certain level of awareness. But it would be lovely to have someone who you feel is objective but who has the skills to question you, challenge you and pull out of you what you really think and feel. Someone who could help you to reflect and develop the depth of understanding that you need to be an effective worker.

(Ann Robinson)

Why should youth workers engage in such a process of self development?

Because youth workers need to establish the 'moral authority' of those who practise what they preach. (Jeffs and Smith 1996:52)

I suppose, in the end, what we are trying to do is to get young people to control themselves through making the right choices. Not just in terms of what we think are the right choices, but the choices that are genuinely in their interest in terms of furthering their well-being. The best way to do that is that we also control ourselves, but you cannot do that unless you have analysed yourself. I think that's one of the most important things you should get from a training situation.

Because youth workers need some basis for resolving the various ethical issues, problems and dilemmas inevitably encountered in their work. (Banks 1999)

One of the problems is knowing what right you've really got to be talking about morals with young people. So, for instance, how can you talk with them about not taking drugs and then go off for a drink at the end of the evening with the other workers. I know that alcohol can be as harmful as any of these other drugs. Therefore, who am I to say 'I'd rather you didn't do that' when I know that, if that young man said to me 'I'd rather you didn't go to the pub', I wouldn't take any notice of him.

Because youth work demands it.

Youth work is about respect. It's about recognising and valuing young people. It's about challenge. It's actually about working from that particular value base which is, in itself, a problem because, firstly, we have difficulties in the articulation of those values, and secondly, for many people, in their careers in Wales, they don't know that those values exist. And that's because there has been a very traditional route in people becoming youth workers in Wales, and people becoming youth officers in Wales which is actually around teacher training. There is an overwhelming number of people in Wales who are teacher trained. And actually having an opportunity to explore, challenge, question, debate; to analyse the value base of youth work, is something that they have never had the opportunity to do.

Because, as Aristotle noted, the 'fundamental moral and intellectual activities that go to make up a flourishing life cannot be continuously engaged in with pleasure and interest unless they are engaged in as part of shared activities with others who are themselves morally good persons'. (Cited in Cooper 1980: 331)

We live here and draw our strength from being a part of this community. We are known in the community and, in holding true to our values, we have earned the respect accorded to those who genuinely care about the neighbourhood and it's people.

Because wisdom brings virtue and virtue brings happiness. (Socrates)

It's about honesty. If I can't be honest in the work relationship. If I have to suppress myself then I don't want to be involved in it. For me, it's as much about me as it is about the work, because I like to feel that my work is an expression of me. It's my creativity and I have integrity within that. So I don't want to be involved in something that's going to diminish my integrity. Just doing something for the sake of doing it isn't part of my value system.

Because it is our human responsibility: 'the only worthwhile thing a person can do is to become as good a person as possible'. (Confucius)

Youth work is about making a human-to-human connection with young people, and that adds a kind of spiritual dimension to the relationship. By this I mean a deep appreciation of humanness – of human beings contacting each other in a way that isn't based on who the other person is – just based on the fact that they are human and no other criteria. That the person has intrinsic value because they are another human being on the planet. That's not easy, but I think it can be taught, given reasonable raw material – that is, a worker who has some spiritual sense or value base of their own.

In the process, workers will need to:

- Overcome their selfishness.
- Gain an awareness of the roots of their fears (of life or uncertainty), their sense of powerlessness, distrust of people 'and the many other subtle roots that have grown together so thickly that it often is impossible to uproot them'.
- Change their practice.
- 'Go out of oneself' into the world outside of one's own ego. (Fromm 1993:119)

For, in the end, true knowledge of oneself and others is liberating and conducive to well-being. (Fromm, 1993:86)

Conclusion

The main argument of this book is that 'youth work' is a distinct activity in its own right and different from other forms of work with young people – not because of its methods, 'curriculum' content or 'target groups', but because of its 'core' purpose.

The police, social workers, teachers all work with young people. But that's not necessarily in a way that I would see as promoting the value base of youth work or the code of ethics that is the driving force of youth work. The main difference is that teachers see young people as pupils. Doctors see young people as patients. Probation officers and social workers see young people as clients. Whereas the youth service sees young people as people. That is, we are focused on young people and where they are and what they are thinking about. And we are involved in that process at different levels, with different people in different places without the hard curriculum of schools, say, where you have to turn young people out to achieve a particular thing at a particular time in their life.

The problem is that the Sports Council wants young people to get involved in sport. The Arts Council wants young people to get involved in the arts. The health service want us to stop teenage pregnancies. The police want young people to stop committing crime. The housing department don't want young people causing offence to old age pensioners. The list is endless. Now these agencies are all looking to the youth service to control young people in these different aspects. The poor youth worker, though, is coming from a place that's about educating people. Admittedly, that educative process would lead to young people thinking about their behaviour in those different arenas, but it wouldn't be focused on hitting those targets specifically.

Young people come to us because they want to. If we don't have a positive effect on young people, they don't come back. So they may come because they are in crisis. They may come for an activity. Or they may come just for you, because you enable them to think about, and feel positive about, themselves. Whereas the agenda of teaching is not necessarily about young people getting to know themselves. It is about young people getting to know knowledge that is external to them.

Partnership

But youth work does not happen in isolation, and the youth service is not an island unto itself. Neither should it be. Indeed, 'high performing authorities' not only 'have a service identity which centres on young people and the partnership with them…[which]…permeates all aspects of their work', but also contribute to cross-agency youth strategy and strategic partnerships, which support joint planning, development and provision. (Marken, Perrett and Wylie 1998)

The benefits of partnership initiatives can be identified as:

- Increased capacity to attract funding.
- Enhancement of the youth service's ability to provide experiences and opportunities for young people.
- Increased capacity of the youth service to support responsiveness of other agencies to the needs of young people.
- Improvement in the integration of services to young people.

However:

Multi-agency work is good because you can ensure that particular services are offered to young people. That can work well as long as everyone is committed to working with each other, and they have a common goal which amounts to more than just doing it because we can get the funding. We need to be doing it because we all believe in young people, and their right to have a chance to explore their values, or grow and develop and meet other young people, and have different experiences.

Actually, as a voluntary organisation, we get more funding if we go for partnership money. But the problem with that is that you have to compromise your values. I've seen some organisations change their whole methodology and style in order to get money. I'm not saying that this agency hasn't been tempted, but it's a bit like selling yourself to the devil, whether that's about the ratio of staff to young people or around equality issues. I like partnerships that are based on true voluntary relationships and where people are equal partners.

So there are benefits to be gained from partnership work and there are also dangers. Significantly, these involve the question of shared goals, whether or not the youth service organisation is perceived as 'the agent' of the other partner(s), the extent to which youth work organisations end up compromising their values, and the issue of which (organisational) culture will prevail. In entering into cross-departmental or cross-agency partnerships, youth services and youth work organisations, therefore, need to be clear about their aims and underpinning values. Lack of such clarity could simply result in the youth service pursuing the agenda of other agencies. A tendency which is already becoming all too familiar.

> *You have to be careful about the assumptions made by other agencies about what they think you are about. For example, we do some joint work with the local school, with whom we share a client group, and I think that there was some expectation on their part that we are sort of their agents, so we have had to be quite quick to say 'No. This is what we are doing and this is what you are doing' and pointing out that these were different and separate things even though we were working together.*

> *The key thing about having a youth service is that it is called a youth service and is, therefore, there to service young people. Probation service is a law and order service. Social service is about the social welfare aspects of young people's lives. That's not to say that these other services don't work effectively with young people in their own way, but, in terms of partnership, the question is whose values and culture will prevail? For example, the youth service is currently talking about seconding a youth worker to youth justice. Why not have a youth justice worker seconded to the youth service? In that way, they will be working within a youth work culture with youth work values as opposed to the other way around. The important thing is that in any partnership the youth service needs to be clear about it's aims and what it's values are, and not just see itself as pursuing the other agencies' agenda.*

> *I don't know what's happening with the mainstream youth service, really. It just feels like something is slipping and that the focus of the work is just getting to be more about money and just doing projects because you can get the funding. The result is that we're getting more and more work around crime prevention and teenage pregnancy and things like that. Not that I think that work isn't important, but sometimes I just question what the motivation is behind it.*

Key questions

Before engaging into partnerships, youth service organisations therefore need to ask themselves a number of key questions.

- Will the partnership benefit the young people and communities you exist to serve, or will it distract you from your core aims?
- What do you hope to achieve through the partnership?
- Will your intentions, purpose and values be compromised?
- Is there a common vision and sufficient common ground amongst the partners?

- Is there enough mutual respect to allow negotiation over aims, issues, values and concerns?
- Is there sufficient 'know-how' to manage partnership initiatives and affairs?
- What is your input – resources, knowledge skills?
- What role(s) do you want to play? (adapted from Wilson and Charlton 1998)

> *We do ourselves a disservice I think, as youth workers, in that, because we are always chasing money, we end up with all sorts of partners because of the way funding bids are structured. Often, it's just a case of the more partners you have the better, so the youth service gets a call. Far too often, because these initiatives come via other routes into local authority – the schools stuff, disaffected youth, the crime concern stuff – it's often the last minute that youth work gets involved. It's down the line instead of it coming the other way, where the youth service is in the position of deciding whether it wants to work with the police, or probation, or whoever. In the process, youth services haven't stood back and said 'Yes, we'll be involved in this project but we want a particular role, or we want to be there as a major partner, or even leading.' Now we are getting cases where the youth service is specifically mentioned in these partnership arrangements, it is even more important for the service to be able to say what it's about and what it can offer. And that understanding of what youth work can do is obviously for the youth service to clarify.*

What is youth work?

This book opened with the assertion that the future of youth work (and the youth service) rests, not on its ability to successfully pursue the agendas and objectives of other agencies, but on the clear articulation of its own 'core' purpose and intended outcomes.

It goes on to argue that the purpose of youth work is to engage with young people in the process of moral philosophising, through which they make sense of themselves and the world. Not as a side effect, or 'added value', but as the essential foundation on which the observable approaches to youth work are built.

As such, the youth work **process** is envisioned as a process of reflection and self examination through which young people increasingly integrate their values, actions and identity; and take charge of themselves as empowered human beings. Youth work, therefore, enables and supports young people to:

- explore their values
- deliberate on the principles of their own moral judgements
- make reasoned choices that can be sustained through committed action

In the process, young people learn and develop:

- The skills of critical thinking and rational judgement – which enable them to make reasoned choices and informed decisions.
- The ability to engage in 'moral inquiry' – about what is 'good' and conducive to the 'good life' generally.
- A disposition towards virtue (adherence to moral and ethical standards) – as a central feature of their identity and their responsibility as social beings in a social world.

What do youth workers do?

What youth workers do is make 'relationships' with young people which accept and value young people; and demonstrate honesty, trust, respect and reciprocity. And, through such relationships, motivate and inspire young people to engage in the process of moral deliberation and learning from experience which supports their:

- personal development and well-being (of body, mind and spirit)
- autonomous informed decision making
- active participation
- critical involvement in their community and society

In order to successfully undertake such work, youth workers must themselves engage in a process of philosophical reflection. A process of training and development which enables **them** to develop the skills of critical thinking, through participation in disciplined discussions about values and moral principles, and the practice of virtue, through their own action, reflection and learning.

The very nature of such an endeavour means that it is not 'value free', since virtue cannot be reduced simply to 'feelings' or personal preference, particularly in a society where 'we are in danger of seeing pluralism and the existence of different values as a virtue in itself, producing an insidious slide from the fact of cultural pluralism to the supposed fact of ethical relativism. (Boyd 1992:144) The challenge for youth workers and the youth service is how to develop a youth work practise which:

- Develops the potential for excellence in each individual, whilst also serving the 'common good'.
- Promotes the noblest life for the individual, while encouraging 'civic courage'.
- Affirms the uniqueness of each person, while acknowledging and confronting the structural inequalities and institutionalised oppressions, which advantage some groups of people at the expense of others, and which tip the balance of power in ways which act to dominate rather than liberate.

Art of youth work

The approach outlined in this book provides the fundamental scheme for just such a practice. A practice based not on the need to address current social problems and political priorities, but on a commitment to developing the truly lifelong goals of rational judgement and authentic human existence. For it is in encouraging these potentialities in young people that they will be supported to take charge of themselves and the meanings they compose for their lives.

Moral philosophy is, however, not an exact science (Aristotle 1987:11). It is, therefore, for each of us to judge the worthiness and relevance of what is written here against our own experience, knowledge and understanding.

And, finally, to borrow from the words of Benedict De Spinoza (1989:278):

> *If the way which I have pointed out seems exceedingly hard, it can nevertheless be achieved. Indeed, it must be difficult as we have yet to grasp it. And were the task easier, it would not have eluded us for so long. But all things excellent are as difficult as they are rare.*

Bibliography

Advisory Group on Citizenship (1998). *Education for Citizenship and the Teaching of Democracy in Schools*. London: Qualifications and Curriculum Authority.

Aristotle (384–322 BC). *The Nicomachean Ethics*. Translated by Welldon, J. (1987). Buffalo, NY: Promethus Books.

Bandura, A. (Ed.) (1974). *Psychological Modelling: Conflicting Theories*. New York: Lieber-Atherton.

Banks, S. (1995). *Ethics and Values in Social Work*. London: Macmillan.

Banks, S. (1997). The Dilemmas of Intervention. In Roche, J., and Tucker, S. (Eds.). *Youth In Society*. London: Sage.

Banks, S. (Ed.) (1999). *Ethical Issues in Youth Work*. London: Routledge.

Barnes, L.J. (1948). *The Outlook for Youth Work*. London: King George's Jubilee Trust.

Barrow, R. (1975). *Moral Philosophy for Education*. London: Allen & Unwin Ltd.

Barrow, R. (1981). *The Philosophy of Schooling*. Brighton: Wheatsheaf Books Ltd.

Becsky, S., and Perrett, J. (1999). *Youth Policy and Youth Services in the United Kingdom*. Leicester: IJAB/NYA.

Benn, S., and Peters, R. (1959). *Social Principles and the Democratic State*. London: Allen & Unwin.

Bentham, J. (1748–1832). *Introduction to the Principles of Morals and Legislation*, (1948). Oxford: Basil Blackwell.

Berger, P., and Luckman, T. (1967). *The Social Construction of Reality*. Harmondsworth: Penguin.

Bloxham, S. (1997). The Social Contract Between Young People and Society. In Ledgerwood, I., and Kendra, N. (Eds.). *The Challenge of the Future*. Lyme Regis: Russell House Publishing.

Board of Education

(1939). *In The Service of Youth (Circular 1486)*. London: HMSO (now available in *Documents of Historical Importance* (1982). National Youth Bureau).

(1940). *The Challenge of Youth (Circular 1516)*. London: HMSO (now available in *Documents of Historical Importance* (1982) NYB).

Bolger, S., and Scott, D. (1984). *Starting From Strengths – Report of the Panel to Promote the Continuing Development and Training for Part-time and Voluntary Youth and Community Workers.* Leicester: National Youth Bureau.

Booton, F. (1985). *Studies in Social Education. Vol 1: 1860–1890.* Hove: Benfield Press.

Boyd, D. (1992). The Moral Part of Pluralism as the Plural Part of Moral Education. In Power, F., and Lapsley, D. (Eds.). *Education, Politics and Values: The Challenge of Pluralism.* London: University of Notre Dame Press.

Brabeck, M. (1993). Moral Judgement: Theory and Research on Differences Between Males and Females. In Larrabee (Ed.). *An Ethic of Care.* London: Routledge.

Brew, J., Macalister (1957). *Youth and Youth Groups.* London: Faber and Faber.

Brookfield, S. (1987). *Developing Critical Thinkers.* Milton Keynes: Open University Press.

Burke, T., and Loewenstein, P. (1998). Me and My Shadow. In *Young People Now.* Issue 107, March 1998: pp 32–33.

Clutterbuck, D., and Sweeney, J. (1997). *Coaching and Mentoring.* London: Clutterbuck Palmer Schneider Ltd.

Coleman, J., and Hendry, L. (1990). *The Nature of Adolescence.* London: Routledge.

Coleman, J. (1992). The Nature of Adolescence. In Coleman, J., and Warren-Adamson, C. (Eds.). *Youth Policy in the 1990s: The Way Forward.* London: Routledge.

Coleman, J., Catan, L., and Dennison, C. (1997). You're the Last Person I'd Talk to. In Roche, J., and Tucker, S. (Eds.). *Youth in Society.* London: Sage.

Confucius (551–479 BC) *The Analects.* Translated by Lau, D.C. (1979). Harmondsworth: Penguin.

Cooper, J. (1980). Aristotle on Friendship. In Rorty, A. (Ed.). *Essays on Aristotle's Ethics.* Los Angeles: University of California Press.

Cortazzi, M. (1993). *Narrative Analysis.* London: The Falmer Press

Crimmens, D., and Whalen, A. (1999). Rights Based Approaches to Work with Young People. In Banks, S. (Ed.). *Ethical Issues in Youth Work.* London: Routledge

Davies, B., and Gibson, A. (1967). *The Social Education of the Adolescent.* London: University of London Press.

De Silva, P. (1993). Buddhist Ethics. In Singer, P. (Ed.). *A Companion To Ethics.* Oxford: Blackwell.

Dewey, J. (1961). *Democracy and Education: An Introduction to the Philosophy of Education.* New York: Macmillan.

Eby, L. (1997). Alternative Forms of Mentoring in Changing Organisational Environments: A Conceptual Extension of the Mentoring Literature. In *Journal of Vocational Behaviour.* Issue 51: pp 125–144.

ECOTEC Research and Consulting Ltd (1997). *Survey of Careers Service Work with Disaffected Young People.* London: Department for Education and Employment.

Eggleston, J. (1976). *Adolescence and Community: The Youth Service in Britain.* London: Edward Arnold.

Ennis, R. (1962). A Concept of Critical Thinking: A Proposed Basis for Research in the Teaching and Evaluation of Critical Thinking Ability. In *Harvard Educational Review.* Vol 32(1): pp 81–111.

Everitt, A., Hardiker, P., Littlewood, J., and Mullender, A. (1992). *Applied Research for Better Practice.* London: Macmillan.

Fisher, A. (1991). Critical Thinking. In Coles, M., and Robinson, W. (Eds.). *Teaching Thinking.* Bristol: Bristol Classical Press.

Foucault, M. (1988). Technologies of the Self. In Martin, L., Gutman, H., and Hutton, P. (Eds.). *Technologies of the Self.* London: Tavistock.

Franklin, A., and Franklin, B. (1990). Age and Power. In Jeffs, T., and Smith, M. (Eds.) *Young People, Inequality and Youth Work.* London: Macmillan.

Freire, P. (1972). *Pedagogy of the Oppressed.* Harmondsworth: Penguin.

Freire, P. (1976). *Education: The Practice of Freedom.* London: Writers and Readers Publishing Cooperative.

Fromm, E. (1993). *The Art of Being.* London: Constable.

Giddens, A. (1991). *Modernity and Self Identity.* Cambridge: Polity Press.

Gilligan, C. (1982). *In a Different Voice.* Cambridge, MA: Harvard University Press.

Gottlieb, A. (1997). *Socrates.* London: Phoenix.

Green, M., and Christian, C. (1998). *Accompanying Young People on the Spiritual Path.* London: The National Society/Church House Publishing.

Hardy, C., Lawrence, B., and Phillips, N. (1998). Talk and Action: Conversations and Narrative in Interorganizational Collaboration. In Grant, D., Keenoy, T., and Oswick, C. (Eds.) (1998). *Discourse and Organisation.* London: Sage.

HMSO

(1944) *Teachers and Youth Leaders: Report of the Committee Appointed by the Board of Education to Consider the Supply, Recruitment and Training of Teachers and Youth Leaders* (The McNair Report).

(1960) *The Youth Service in England and Wales*, Albemarle Committee.

(1969) *Youth and Community Work in the 70s*, Milson-Fairbairn Committees.

(1982) *Experience and Participation*, Thompson Committee.

Hume, D. (1738). *Treatise of Human Nature*. Selby-Bigge, L., and Nidditch, P. (Eds.) (1978). Oxford: Clarendon Press.

Hunter, R., Payne, B., Pittham, P., and Young, K. (1999). *Something to Say*. Leicester: Youth Work Press.

Jackson, M., Bolger, S., and Young, K. (1989). *Handbook for Personal Training Advisers*. Leicester: Council for Education and Training in Youth and Community Work.

Jeffs, T., and Smith, M. (1996). *Informal Education – Conversation, Democracy and Learning*. Derby: Education Now Publishing Co-operative Limited.

Jeffs, T., and Smith, M. (1998). The Problem of 'Youth' for Youth Work. In *Youth and Policy*. Issue 62, Winter 1998/99: pp 45–66.

Jeffs, T., and Smith, M. (1999). Resourcing Youth Work: Dirty Hands and Tainted Money. In Banks, S. (Ed.). *Ethical Issues in Youth Work*. London: Routledge.

Kant, I. (1785). *Groundwork of the Metaphysic of Morals*. Translated by Paton, H.J. (1948). *The Moral Law*. New York: Harper Torchbooks

Kellner, M. (1993). Jewish Ethics. In Singer, P. (Ed.). *A Companion To Ethics*. Oxford: Blackwell

Khema, A. (1987). *Being Nobody, Going Nowhere*. London: Wisdom Publications.

King George's Jubilee Trust (1951). *Youth Service Tomorrow* – A report of a meeting arranged by King George's Jubilee Trust held at Ashridge, 27–30 April 1951.

Kleinig, J. (1982). *Philosophical Issues in Education*. London: Croom Helm.

Kohlberg, L. (1981). *Essays on Moral Development: Vol I The Philosophy of Moral Development*. San Francisco, CA: Harper and Row.

Kohlberg, L. (1983). *Essays on Moral Development: Vol II The Psychology of Moral Development*. San Francisco, CA: Harper and Row.

Kolb, D. (1984). *Experiential Learning*. Englewood Cliffs, NY: Prentice-Hall.

Kosman, L. (1980). Being Properly Affected: Virtues and Feelings in Aristotle's Ethics. In Rorty, A. (Ed.). *Essays on Aristotle's Ethics*. Los Angeles, CA: University of California Press.

Kram, K., and Isabella, L. (1985). Mentoring Alternatives: The Role of Peer Relationships in Career Development. In *Academy of Management Journal*. Issue 28: pp 110–132.

Kupperman, J. (1983). *The Foundations of Morality*. London: Allen & Unwin.

Leighton, J. (1972). *The Principles and Practice of Youth and Community Work*. London: Chester House Publications.

Lipman, M. (1988). *Philosophy Goes To School*. Philadelphia: Temple University Press.

Lorenz, W. (1996). Pedagogical Principles for Anti-racist Strategies. In Aluffi-Pentini, A., and Lorenz, W. (Eds.). *Anti-racist Work with Young People*. Lyme Regis: Russell House Publishing Ltd.

MacIntyre, A. (1985) (2nd edition). *After Virtue: A Study in Moral Theory*. London: Duckworth.

MacIntyre, A. (1988). *Whose Justice? Which Rationality?* London: Duckworth.

Mackie, J. (1990). *Ethics: Inventing Right and Wrong*. Harmondsworth: Penguin.

Marken, M., Perrett, P., and Wylie, T. (1998). *England's Youth Service – The 1998 Audit*. Leicester: Youth Work Press.

Marshak, R. (1998). A Discourse on Discourse: Redeeming the Meaning of Talk. In Grant, D., Keenoy, T., and Oswick, C. (Eds.). *Discourse and Organisation*. London: Sage.

Mencius. [The] *Mencius*. Translated by Lau, D.C. (1970). Harmondsworth: Penguin. (Mencius was probably born a century or so after the death of Confucius and likely to have died by the end of the fourth century BC. The Mencius was written in the years just after 320 BC.)

Midgley, M. (1997). Can Education Be Moral? In Smith, R., and Standish, P. (Eds.). *Teaching Right and Wrong: Moral Education in the Balance*. Stoke on Trent: Trentham Books.

Ministry of Education

    (1943) *The Youth Service After the War*, Youth Advisory Council. London: HMSO.

    (1945) *The Purpose and Content of the Youth Service: A Report of the Youth Advisory Council appointed by the Minister of Education in 1943*. London: HMSO.

Morgan, S., and Banks, S. (1999). The Youth Worker as Confidant. In Banks, S. (Ed.). *Ethical Issues in Youth Work*. London: Routledge

Morrow, V., and Richards, M. (1996). *Transition to Adulthood*. York: Joseph Rowntree Foundation,

Nanji, A. (1993). Islamic Ethics. In Singer, P. (Ed.). *A Companion To Ethics*. Oxford: Blackwell.

NACYS (1989). *Directions for the Youth Service: A Position Paper*. London: Department of Education and Science.

National Youth Agency

    (1997a) *Youth Service Statement of Purpose* – produced by a working group including representatives from the Standing Conference of Principal Youth and Community Officers, National Association of Youth and Community Education Officers, Community and Youth Workers Union, National Council for Voluntary Youth

Services, British Youth Council, Council of Local Education Authorities, Office of Standards in Education, Training Agencies Group and the National Youth Agency. February 1997.

(1997b) *Mentoring* – briefing paper, November 1997.

(1997c) *Professional Endorsement of Qualifying Training in Youth and Community Work.* Leicester: National Youth Agency.

(1998) *Invest in Futures – A Blueprint for Young People's Social Inclusion.* Leicester: NYA.

(1999) *National Occupational Standards for Youth Work: Draft for Consultation*, (valid until 26th February 1999). Leicester: NYA.

National Youth Bureau (1991). *Towards a Core Curriculum – The Next Step: Report of the Second Ministerial Conference*, written by Kerry Young on behalf of the National Conferences Steering Committee. Leicester: NYB.

Noe, R. (1988). An Investigation of the Determinants of Successful Assigned Mentoring Relationships. In *Personnel Psychology.* Issue 41: pp 457–479.

Paraskeva, J. (1992). Youth Work and Informal Education. In Coleman, J., and Warren-Adamson, C. (Eds.). *Youth Policy in the 1990s.* London: Routledge.

Peters, R. (1981). *Moral Development and Moral Education.* London: Allen & Unwin.

Philip, K., and Hendry, L. (1996). Young People and Mentoring – Towards a Typology? In *Journal of Adolescence.* Issue 19: pp 189–201.

Piaget, J. (1932). *The Moral Judgement of the Child.* London: Routledge and Kegan Paul.

Pini, M. (1997). Technologies of the Self. In Roche, J., and Tucker, S. (Eds.). *Youth in Society.* London: Sage.

Plato (c.427–347 BC). *The Dialogues of Plato:* Volume 2 The Symposium and Other Dialogues. Translated by Jowett, B. (1970). London: Sphere Books Limited.

Plato (c.427–347 BC). *The Republic.* Translated by Lee, D. (1974) (2nd edition). Harmondsworth: Penguin.

Preston, R. (1993). Christian Ethics. In Singer, P. (Ed.). *A Companion to Ethics.* Oxford: Basil Blackwell Ltd.

Pring, R. (1984). *Personal and Social Education in the Curriculum.* London: Hodder and Stoughton.

Richardson, J. (1997). The Path to Adulthood and the Failure of Youth Work. In Ledgerwood, I., and Kendra, N. (Eds.). *The Challenge of the Future.* Lyme Regis: Russell House Publishing.

Riessman, C. (1993). *Narrative Analysis.* Newbury Park, CA: Sage.

Robinson, L. (1997). Black Adolescent Identity and the Inadequacies of Western Psychology. In Roche, J., and Tucker, S. (Eds.). *Youth in Society.* London: Sage.

Rokeach, M. (1973). *The Nature of Human Values.* New York: Free Press.

Rorty, A. (1993). Moral Imperialism vs. Moral Conflict: Conflicting Aims of Education. In Darling-Smith, B. (Ed.). *Can Virtue Be Taught?.* Notre Dame: University of Notre Dame Press.

Russell, J., and Adams, D. (1997). The Changing Nature of Mentoring in Organisations: An Introduction to the Special Issue on Mentoring in Organisations. In *Journal of Vocational Behaviour.* Issue 51: pp 1–14.

Saddhatissa, H. (1987). *Buddhist Ethics.* London: Wisdom Publications.

Schneewind, J. (1993). Modern Moral Philosophy. In Singer, P. (Ed.) (1993). *A Companion to Ethics.* Oxford: Basil Blackwell Ltd.

School Curriculum Assessment Authority (1996). *Consultation on Values in Education and the Community,* National Forum for Values in Education and the Community. London: SCAA.

Shotter, J. (1993). *Conversational Realities: Constructing Life Through Language.* London: Sage.

Singer, P. (1997). *How Are We to Live?* Oxford: Oxford University Press.

Smith, D. (1987). *Reshaping the Youth Service.* Leicester: National Youth Bureau.

Smith, M. (1988). *Developing Youth Work.* Milton Keynes: Open University Press.

Spinoza, B., de (1632–1677). *Ethics.* Translated by Elwes R.H.M. (1989). Buffalo, NY: Prometheus Books.

Streng, F. (1993). Cultivating Virtue in a Religiously Plural World: Possibilities and Problems. In Darling-Smith, B. (Ed.). *Can Virtue Be Taught?* Notre Dame: University of Notre Dame Press.

Thompson, N. (1993). *Anti-discriminatory Practice.* London: Macmillan.

United Kingdom Youth Work Alliance (1996). *Agenda For A Generation – Building Effective Youth Work.* Edinburgh: Scottish Community Education Council.

Wainwright, (1996). The Political Transformation of the Health Inequalities Debate. In *Critical Social Poli*cy. Vol. 16(4); Issue 49, November 1996: pp 67–82.

Wallemacq, A., and Sims, D. (1998). The Struggle with Sense. In Grant, D., Keenoy, T., and Oswick, C. (Eds.). *Discourse and Organisation.* London: Sage.

Weick, K. (1995). *Sensemaking in Organisations.* London: Sage Publications.

Whalley, M. (1991). Philosophy for Children. In Coles, M., and Robinson, W. (Eds.). *Teaching Thinking.* Bristol: Bristol Classical Press.

Williams, B. (1993). *Ethics and the Limits of Philosophy.* Hammersmith: Fontana Press.

Williamson, B. (1997). Moral Learning: A Lifelong Task. In Smith, R. and Standish, P. (Eds). *Teaching Right And Wrong: Moral Education in the Balance.* Stoke on Trent: Trentham Books.

Wilson, A., and Charlton, K. (1998). *Making Partnerships Work – A Practical Guide for the Community and Voluntary Sectors*. London: NCVO/Joseph Rowntree Foundation.

Woods, C. (1995). *State of the Queer Nation*. London: Cassell.

Wyn, J., and White, R. (1997). *Rethinking Youth*. London: Sage.

Young Men's Christian Association (1844). In *The YMCA in Focus* (1987).

Young, K. (1998). A Different Agenda? In *Young People Now*. Issue 109, May 1998: pp 34–35.

Young, K. (1999). The Youth Worker as Guide, Philosopher and Friend. In Banks, S. (Ed.). *Ethical Issues in Youth Work*. London: Routledge.